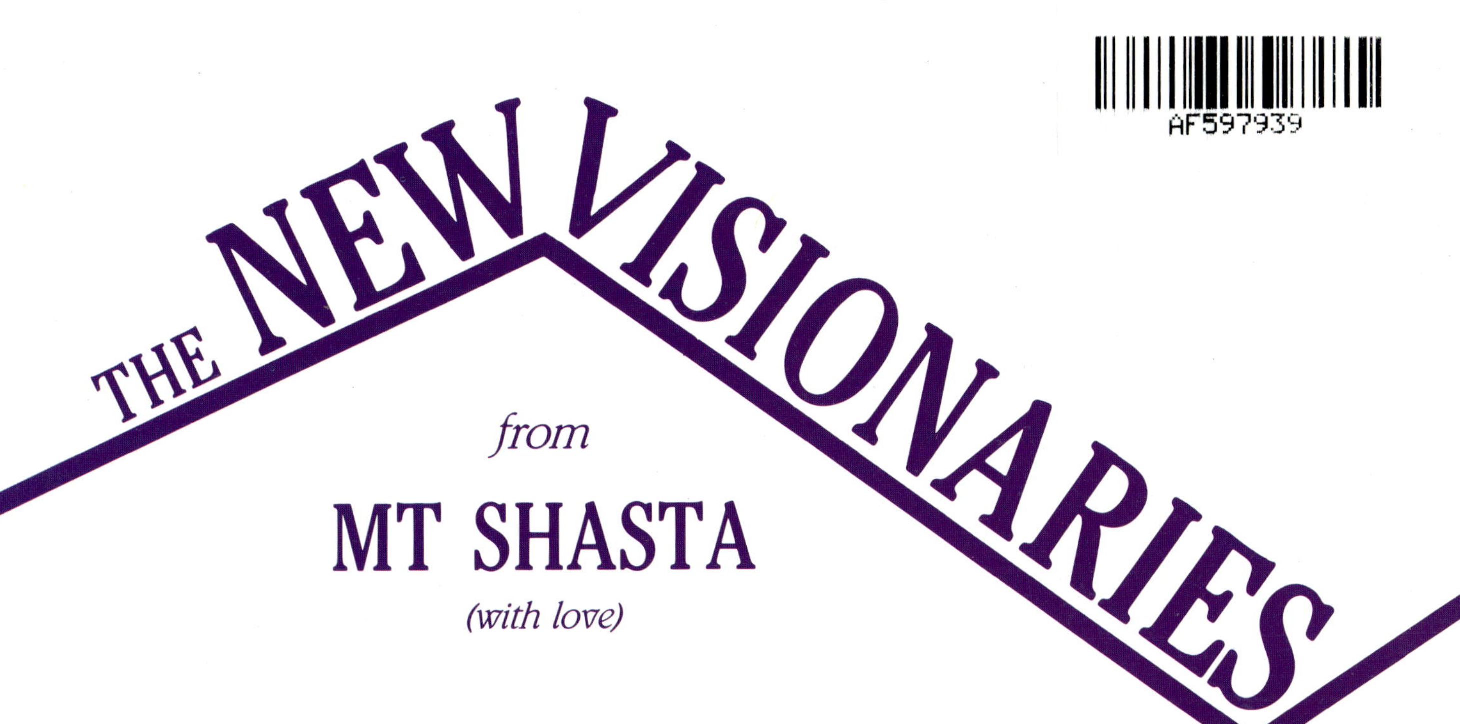

Compiled and Edited by Walter von Finck

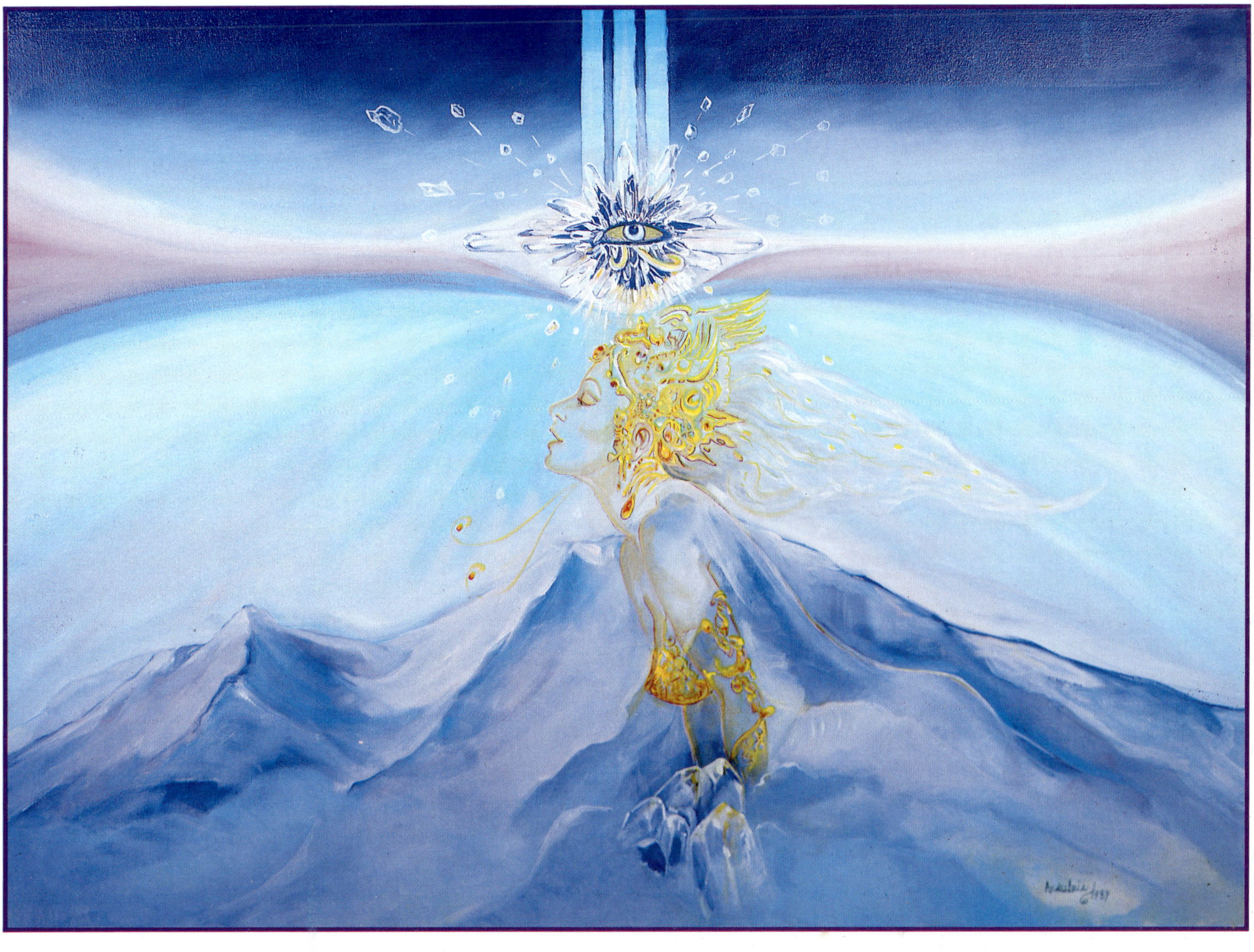

Heartlink '88 30×40 Andraleria

THE NEW VISIONARIES

from Mt. Shasta with Love

Front Cover: *Guardian of Mt. Shasta* by Rodney Birkett
Back Cover: *Cities of Light* by Ixthara

Conceptualized by Ixthara
Typesetting by Bookends and Crystal Castle Graphics
Color separations by Pacific Scanning
Printed in Hong Kong by Union PB & P Press Ltd.

Library of Congress Catalog Number: 89-085586
ISBN: 0-9623960-8-7

For information concerning originals, limited edition prints, posters, and notecards, please write to:

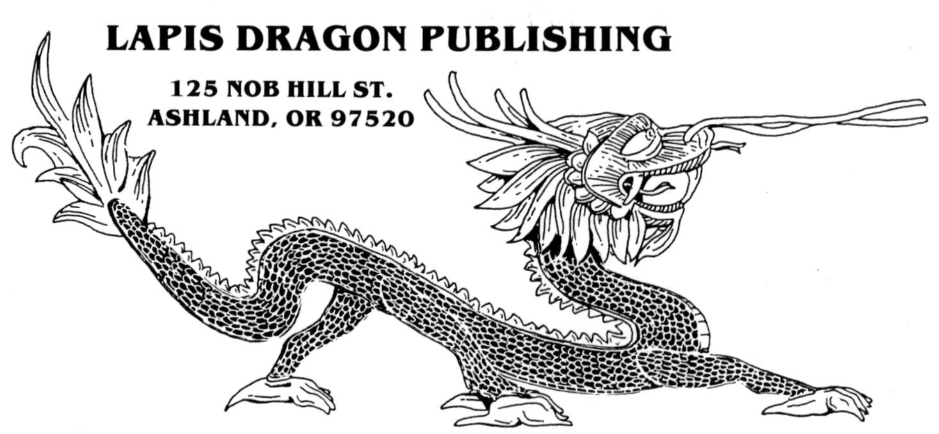

Dance of Light

by Andraleria

Who, if he truly believes in a God, any God, cannot but know that the Infinite Creator must create Beauty that dazzles, illuminates, enchants the senses into Joyous Reverence . . . beyond the wildest imagination.

May I then but touch the hem of that wild and sacred Imagination and be able to transfer some of that exquisite Radiance onto canvas!

In his supreme vanity, man thinks he is the only one—that a Creator who is omniscient, omnipresent and absolute, who has created the very fabric of all that is, has in his supposed lack of vision created only one intelligent life form worth taking seriously.

So man in his supreme vanity, has become afraid to acknowledge the "others" . . . that were in fact created long before and since he was—laughing at them as myth, fantastic and unreal.

Fantastic? Yes!

Unreal? No!

Visionary art comes from the heart. If well executed, it has great power and light. The word "visionary" is well-suited to describe it, for it is just that.

It comes to us in visions from the inner worlds. It comes to us from the light worlds.

Most art is either from the physical plane (copying physical things, like people, landscapes, etc.) or from the subconscious through their art.

Light world impressions can only come into the subtle physical body when it is clear and fairly pure. An artist has had to have lived many lives as an artist as well as many lives of spiritual practice to purify him or herself to be that channel which receives higher visions. Only the pure in heart can receive these visions and of course only the skilled and disciplined can actually manifest them as a physical object, a well-rendered replica of their inner vision. This is not an easy thing to accomplish.

There is also the feeling that is translated through color and movement. Light worlds vibrate with very high frequencies. Their colors are the kind seen in deep meditation and don't come in commercial tubes of paint. They must be created by skill and faith. These subtle colors, pastel or bright, dance a color dance that emits a different radiation which affects not only those who work with them but also those who stand in front of the image and look at it.

The soul responds in joy when it sees its own realms. Our is commonly a dreary world where most people find dull grays and browns the only colors they can handle. The marvelous shimmering paintings of visionary art, full of soul, life actually threaten the matter-immersed personalities of many. Yet there are the others, especially the young, that respond to such paintings, to the colors, to the visions with joy.

Maybe it should be called vibrational art, but then all art is vibrational. What differs is the frequency.

In the study of color's impact on the human psyche and well being, it is known that certain color frequencies act upon the aura of an individual for good and for ill. Browns and grays, drab and ugly, tend to affect the subtle physical body and result in creating low energy fields where depression and ill health are the result.

High keyed colors, pastel and pleasing, have the effect of relaxing, energizing and creating a field of energy where well being is the result.

So powerful are some of these paintings that they can actually heal. This will be a science of the future. If a painting is full of harmony and light, its aura blends with the aura of the observer; the two converge and a healing occurs. This is happening already as many of the visionary artists will confirm.

Monet struggled with light and color and getting prostitutes to pose for him. Visionary artists struggle with translating light and color into higher frequencies, terrestrial forms into celestial ones. It's not as if they can get angels and fairies to pose for them in the studio, even though they know they are there inspiring and guiding them.

Art needs to be felt. The mind should stay out of it, or it becomes like the old story of the Emperor's New Clothes. Everybody "oohed" and "aahed" at what they were led to believe existed, when in truth, as a young child pointed out, he was naked. People are led to believe by volumes of words by the so-called experts that what they are looking at is beautiful, when it may be trash.

Visionary art is here to correct this sad state of affairs. It is too beautiful not to be felt. In time it will bring great art back to the people. Visionary artists are painting possible futures of light and love. Also, they are painting beings that can only be seen through the awakened third eye. They are making their reality more acceptable, they are meshing worlds together.

Visionary art may be one of the most refined ways of spreading Dharma in a world of ever-gathering Darkness.

The human species is very impressionable and it is through visual impressions that the mind and heart are reached the most easily. There is a constant play back and forth between the seen and the manifest.

If all people see is pain, suffering and ugliness, that is all they will aspire to. How great, then, is the responsibility of an artist, especially media artists, as they reach millions.

How poor and empty are their visions!

The few very strong and enlightened souls that have been incarnated to bring some of the Glory of the *real* worlds have an immense task on their hands.

What to them is real is, of course, bizarre to people who can only relate on the painful and drab levels of existence.

These light worlds really do exist and these various beings really do exist. They are not figments of imagination or, rather, they are just that because the imagination is part of the third eye's ability to see into other dimensions. Visionary artists are the warriors bringing images of the light worlds to excite, inspire and build a better future.

The world has not yet received the visionaries with open arms. Yet because they are warriors at heart they hold on to their dreams and their paint brushes.

I feel very privileged to be one of them.

I see a time coming in the not too distant future as the movement gets more exposure when it will expand and the media will take more interest. As the imagery and those ideas and thoughts that stand behind them get more exposure, more light will be able to descend upon humanity and our work shall stand strong.

Visionary artists work on the same frequency, whether we are conscious of it or not. We are, by nature, extremely sensitive, psychic and disciplined. Most people don't realize how disciplined one must be to be an artist of any kind.

The Ancients taught that it takes many life times to become an artist. How many must it take to be an artist of true vision?

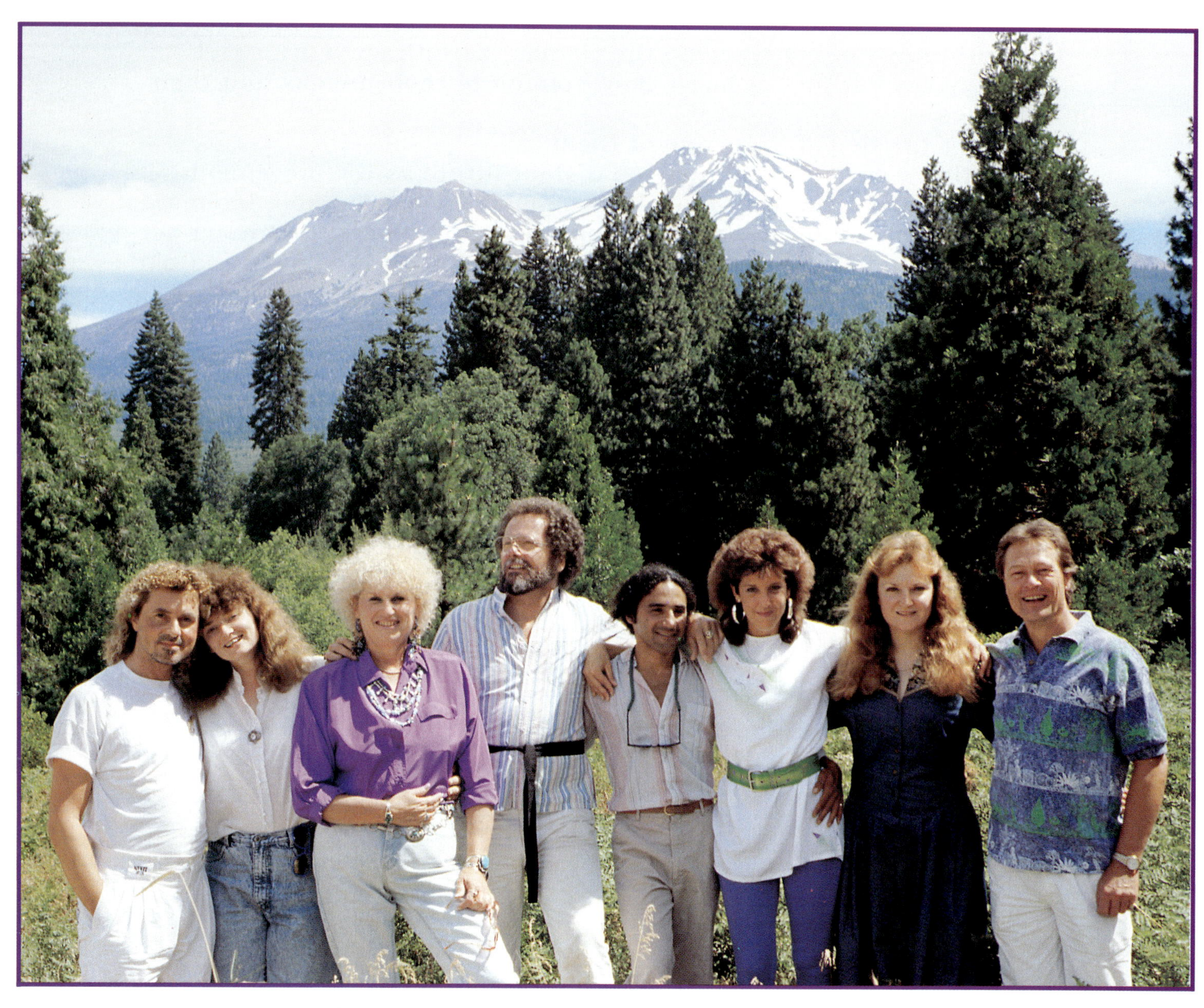

(left to right) Aeoliah, Ixthara, Andraleria, Rodney Birkett, Leonardo Rene, Krystel, Cheryl Yambrach Rose, Walter von Finck.

Paintings by

The purpose of Visionary Art and artists is to make ourselves as receptive a vehicle as possible in order to bring back from the subtler realms high ideals for the planet, by manifesting them on the physical plane. This is the ideal state of the vehicle (the artist) being able to traverse between worlds yet becoming residential to none. It's all about Service to Light.

The major difference between a vision and an idea is: an idea you build on and evolve, while a vision comes through whole and complete. This usually happens in an altered state such as meditation or dreams. For me, New Age music helps create this borderline state where all things are possible, and has become an integral part of my painting process. Of course now they have proved with the help of the electro-encephalagraph that more alpha and theta waves are emitted from the brain while listening to New Age music than with any other type, including classical. I just know it works.

I use high frequency colors sparingly as I am trying to create a pathway and bridge from the mundane consciousness level, or that which is familiar, to the ehteric level. I don't want to bombard all the senses at once, leaving the viewer nothing to do but look. I like to think the viewer will find the path and cross the bridge using what is relative to them individually. Using a realistic palette to begin with creates a departure point where the transition can be made smoothly to the higher realms and to the subtler energies that can heal and nurture. I try to synthesize the two levels in the painting, as in life, where the psychic body and the physical body are fused.

The paintings are done in oil and alkyd on fine linen. I feel the value of the thought should be relfected in the materials.

There is a lot of symbology in my work. I use the rose often as it is an

CHERYL YAMBRACH ROSE

The Hermit
Cheryl Yambrach Rose

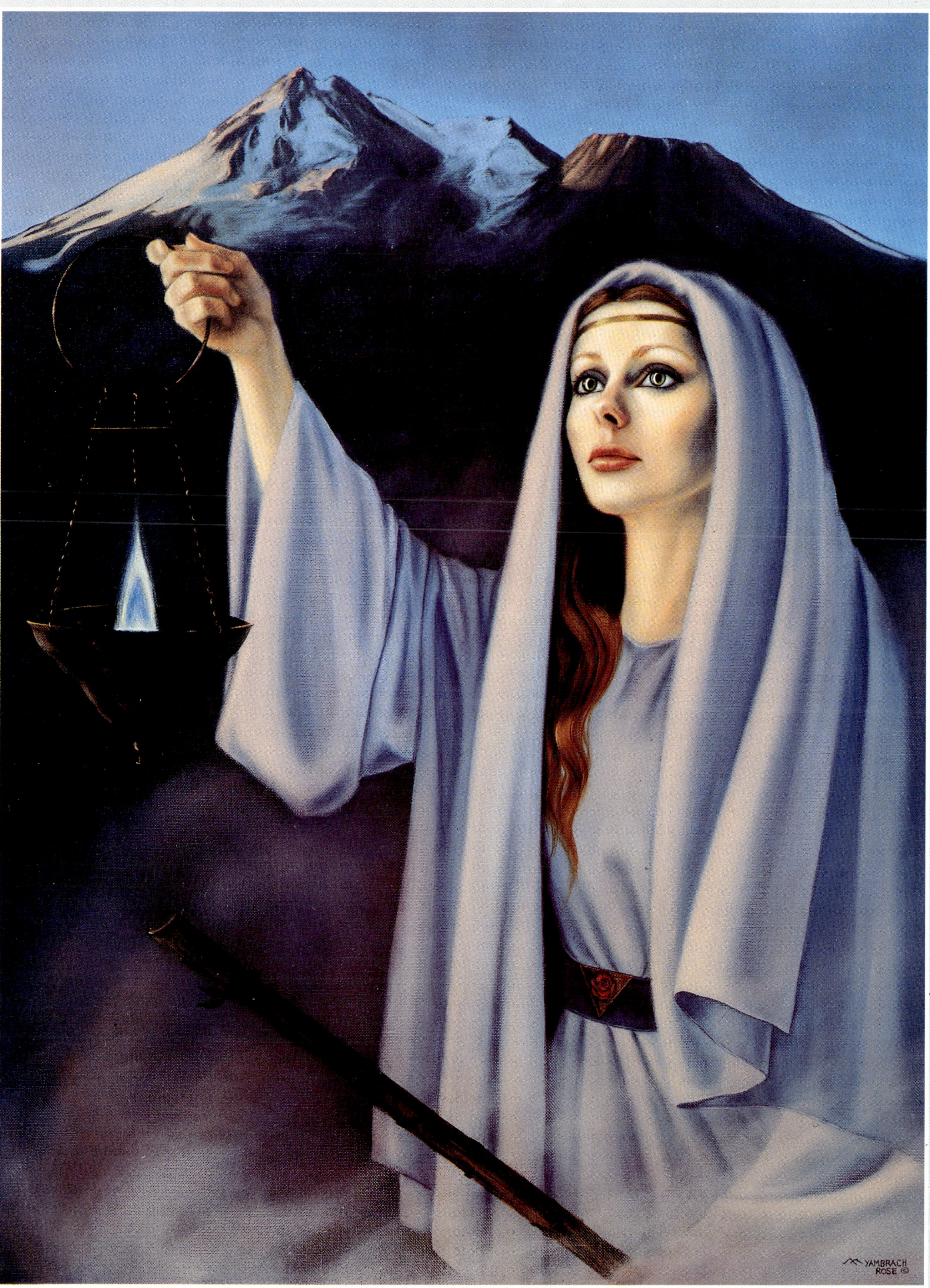
YAMBRACH
ROSE ©

ancient symbol for unfolding enlightenment. The beings I use to express my visions are multidimensional figures that can be historical, or ethereal children of light that are expressing their commitment and purity of purpose.

For example, the painting "The Hermit," the ninth key card of the tarot. The hermit, who is usually depicted as a man, holds the lamp of truth for the stragglers below. Because the Aquarian age is the age of feminine energy, my wise man is a woman. She stands before Mt. Shasta in the dawn light the morning of the convergence. The leaves bursting forth from her staff symbolize the birth of the golden age and the starseed of the child growing within me.

Then on a lighter note, some paintings may express the mere joy of being, such as "Shasta Starflight."

Nicholas Roerich stated long ago that we would attain "peace through culture." He believed that through the nurturing and development of the creative spirit a great artistic awakening would occur, leading to mankind coming into his true evolved state of harmony and peace. Inspired by this, I created a spacebridge painting in 1987 and sent a copy to Mr. Gorbachev. This was partially a value lesson for my daughter. I wanted to show her that the individual can make a difference toward world peace. When we received the letter from the Russian Consulate General that it had been received in Moscow and when she heard Mr. Gorbachev say on TV that he was coming to America because of the letters he had received, she learned that individuals can become a *collective power* and affect and raise the consciousness level of the entire world.

As for personal history, I was born in New York but raised in California. My first conscious realization of my purpose here came in kindergarten. Creation was still a male dominated area at that time, so I remember having to convince the teacher that my place was at the

Shasta Mountain of Light
Cheryl Yambrach Rose

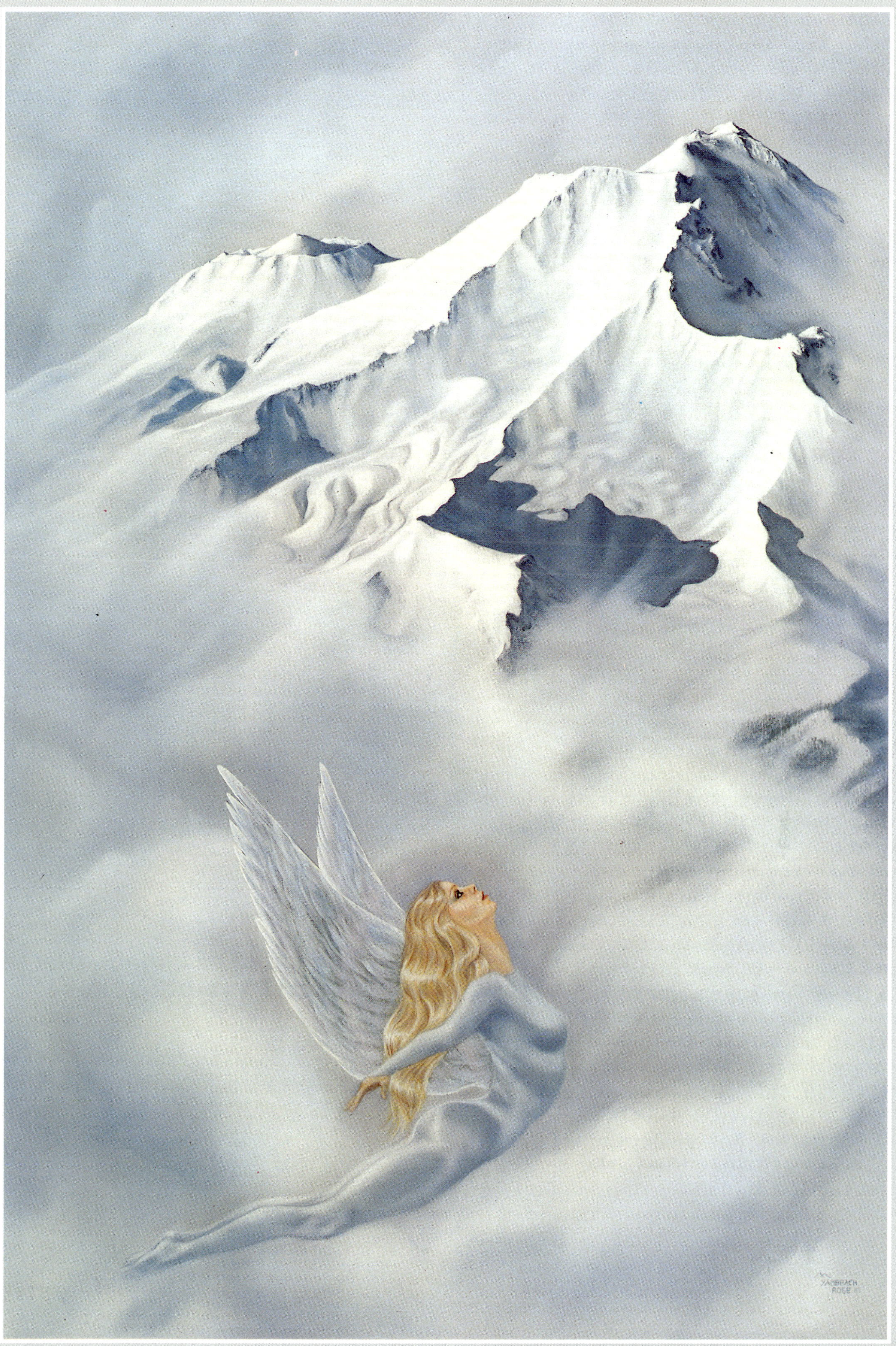
YAMBRACH
ROSE

fingerpainting easels with the boys rather than in the playhouse with the girls. This is symbolic because after attaining my place there—I never left.

I began painting originals in oils at 12 and was represented by two major galleries in the bay area at age 16.

I started with images of people because through them I could best express the emotions and perceptions of my realities.

I earned a degre in painting from an art school, but do not hold it as significant when compared to the actual experience of painting, which acts as a catalyst to the development and heightened awareness of the mind, brain, and objective and psychic senses.

I painted mystical Celtic visions for several years and traveled to Britain to study art and Arthurian archeology in 1976. I was especially inspired by Cornwall and the ruins of Glastonbury. The imagery gathered there still affects my work today.

I took portrait commissions for a couple of years painting all types of people, from rock stars to silicon valley executives.

Moving to Mt. Shasta in 1979, I became involved with Western Art. Living on the old wintering grounds of the Shasta Indians, gave me a feeling of attunement with the ancient spirits that used to live there. I was guided to many sacred ceremonial sights and camps which I documented and painted. I studied with the Shamans and Shastas so I could create using the archetypes and carved symbols that have managed to transcend time and can still be found here. This art was featured in Art West magazine in 1980, the book Contemporary Western Artists, shown at the Favell Museum of Western Art, and in 1984, I was given a reception and show at The Nelson Rockefeller Collection.

Since exploring was easier on horseback, I traded 3 paintings for two Arabian horses and began painting

Threshold of Illumination
Cheryl Yambrach Rose

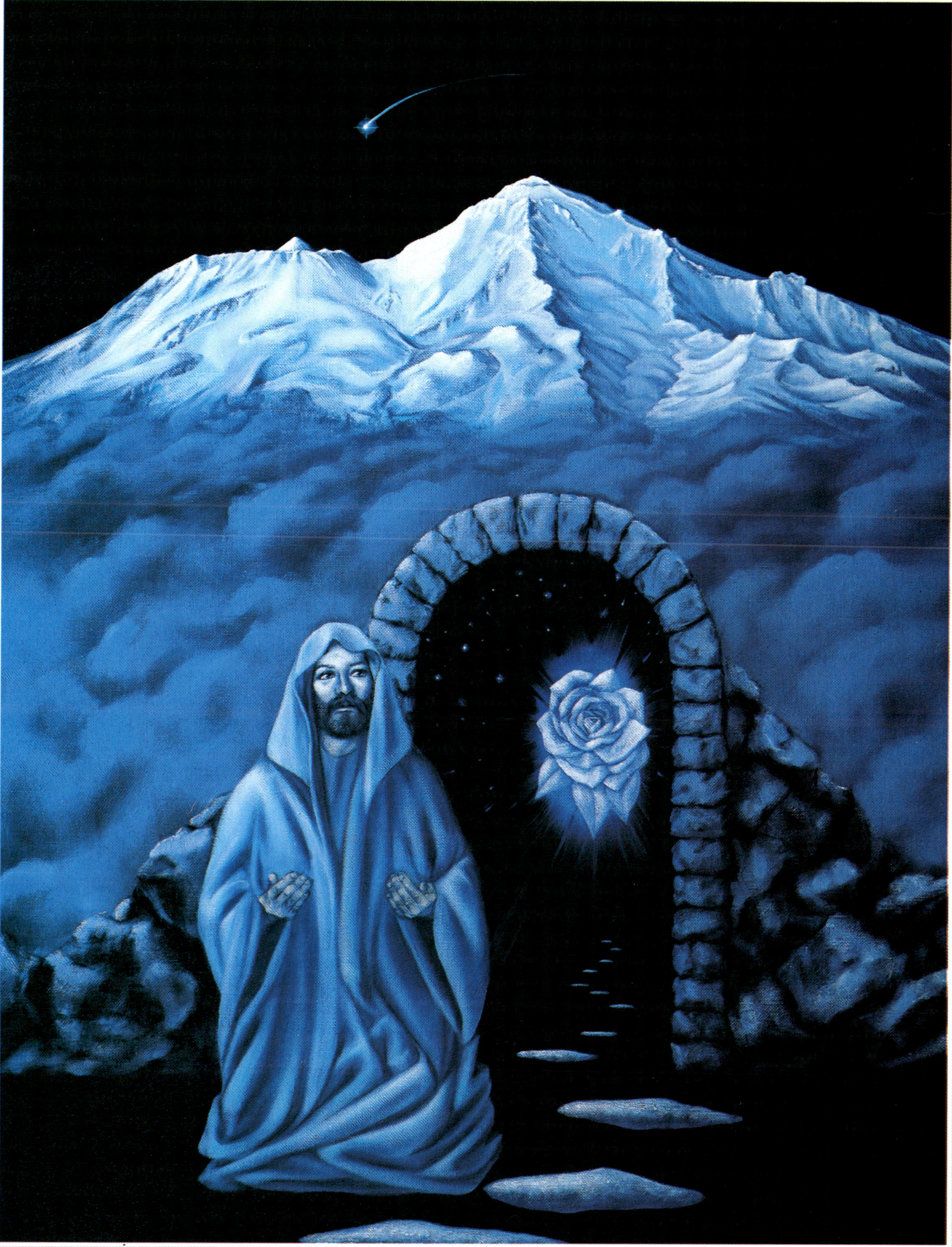

them. This led to doing artwork for the IAHA, and many magazine covers and calendars in Europe, Australia, and the U.S. Always, the mountain loomed ever present as we rode. . . .

I returned to visionary art a few years ago and came home so to speak. I can see where each area of diversification has contributed to the whole—now the paint flows. Recently incorporating Celtic visions with the Shasta work, I feel I have come full circle and the mandala is complete.

Live your Visions,
Love,
Cheryl

The Goddess Awakens (L)
Cheryl Yambrach Rose

Shasta Starflight (R)
Cheryl Yambrach Rose

Celestial Visitation (L)
Cheryl Yambrach Rose

The Initiate (R)
Cheryl Yambrach Rose

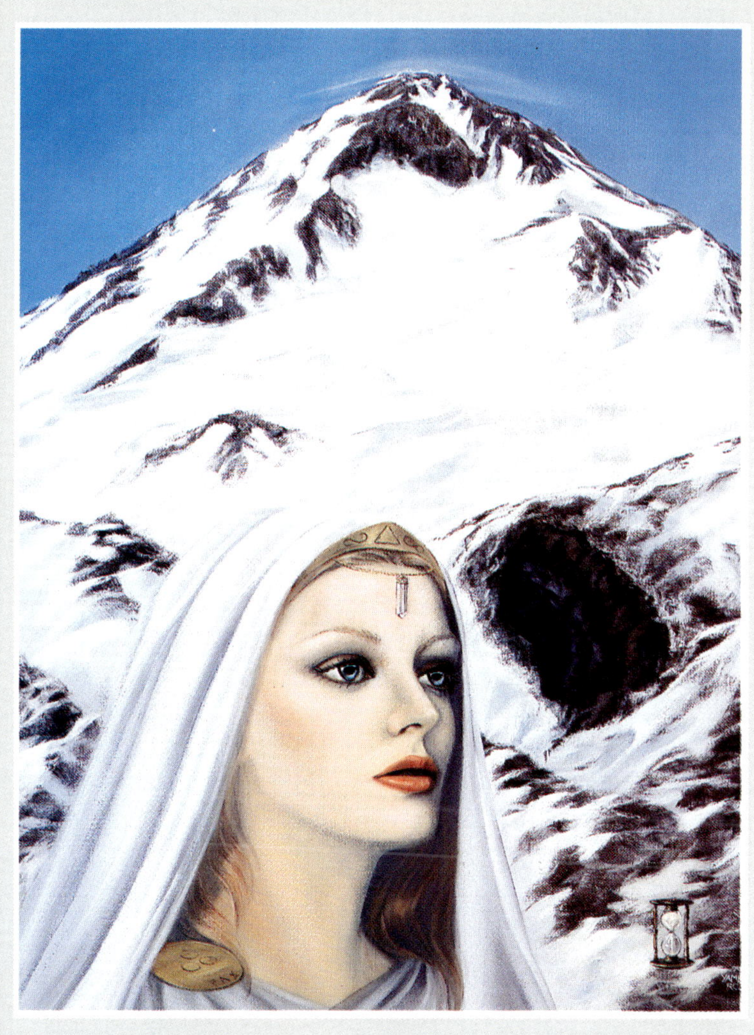

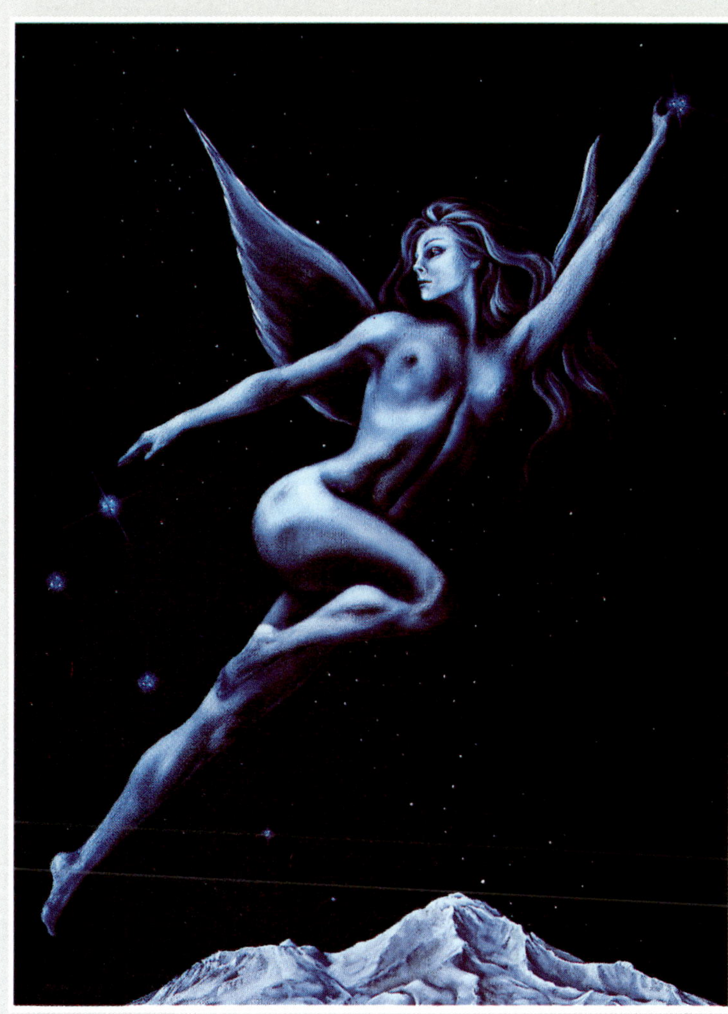

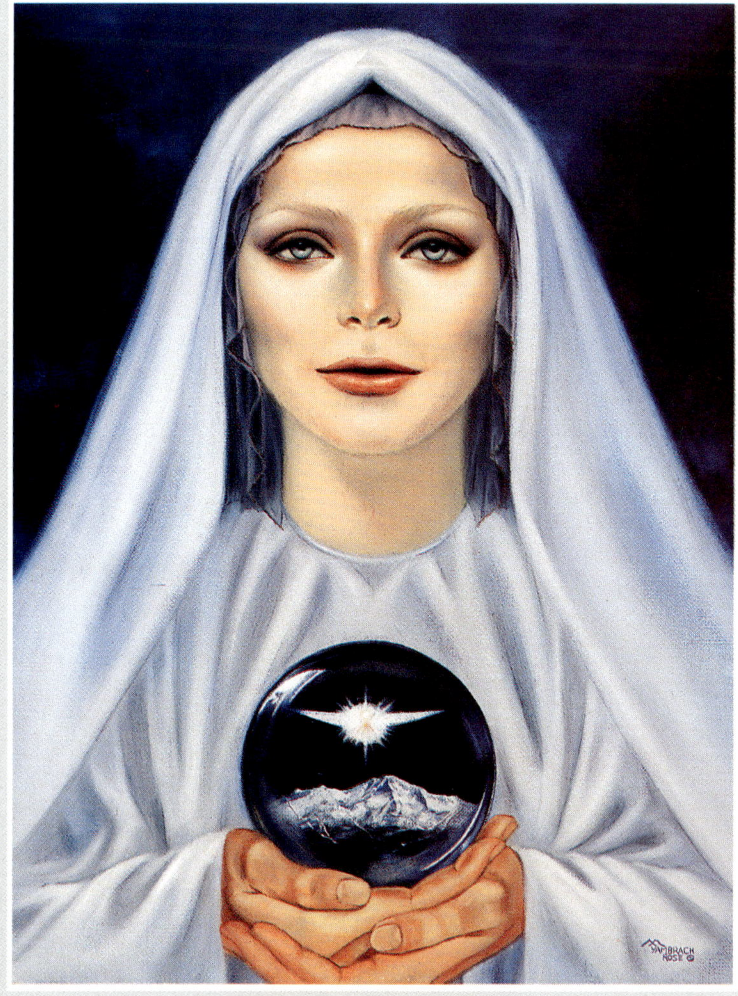
YAMBRACH
ROSE ©

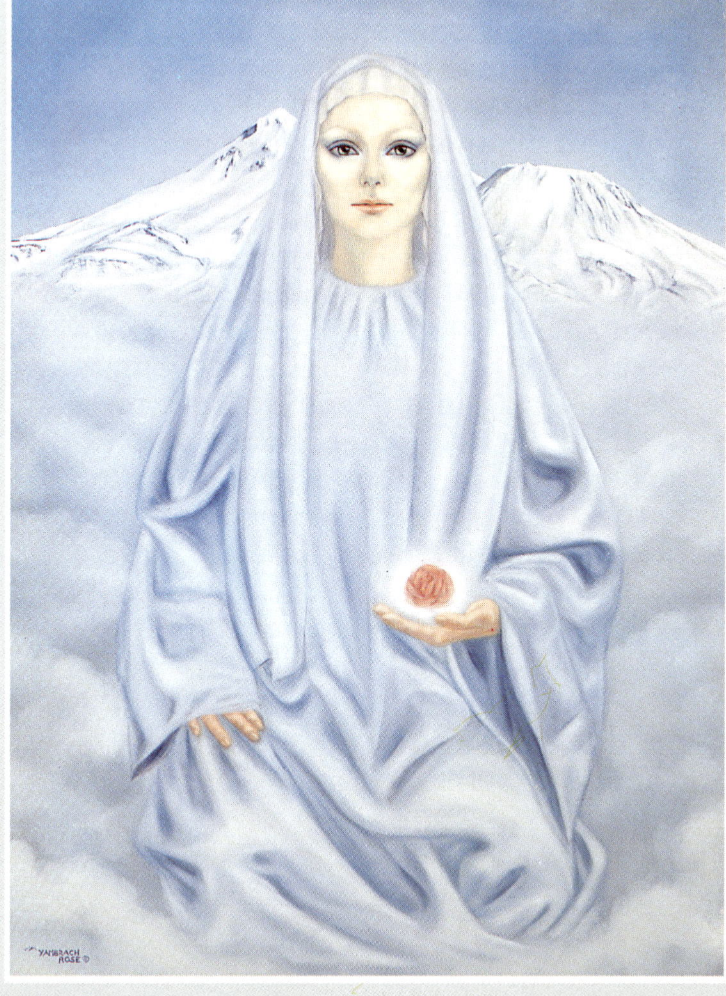
YAMBRACH
ROSE ©

KRYSTEL

Born in Jacksonville, Florida, October 1956, and educated at the Fleming College, Florence Italy, and San Francisco Art Institute, San Francisco, California.

I have exhibited at Cafe Nuvo, San Anselmo, California, 1986; Mind, Body, and Spirit Fair, Honolulu, Hawaii, 1986; The Croissanterie, Honolulu, Hawaii, 1987; The Mystical Ball, Honolulu, Hawaii, 1988; Artifino, Larkspur, California, 1988; and The Crystal Congress, Los Angeles, California, 1988.

I am privately represented by Truth Paradise in Colorado, phone: 303-923-5753; and by Julie Rapkin in Arizona, phone: 602-284-9582.

Beginning in July of 1988 my work has been shown in the following galleries; Mirage Gallery, Sausalito, California, phone: 415-332-8106; and Gallery Obscura, Ashland, Oregon, phone: 503-488-2498.

I create images in the form of Fine Art Paintings and Art For Clothing. These paintings are a guide to higher realms and reflect the love and peace within us all. Painting has become an amazing teacher and ally in my life. Just as I must be open to receive images and allow them to change and evolve I must also 'be there' for life's opportunities and allow myself to change and evolve with them.

By using pure rainbow colors and creating paintings of exquisite beauty I have enhanced and expanded my consciousness. The paintings serve as 'visual affirmations' in an enjoyable way. We are living in an exciting age where we have become much more aware of our environment. Color plays an integral part in how we feel. By surrounding ourselves with beauty we can create a nurturing atmosphere to support us in experiencing all aspects of life harmoniously.

Krystel
415-459-0538

Crystal Spaceship
Krystel

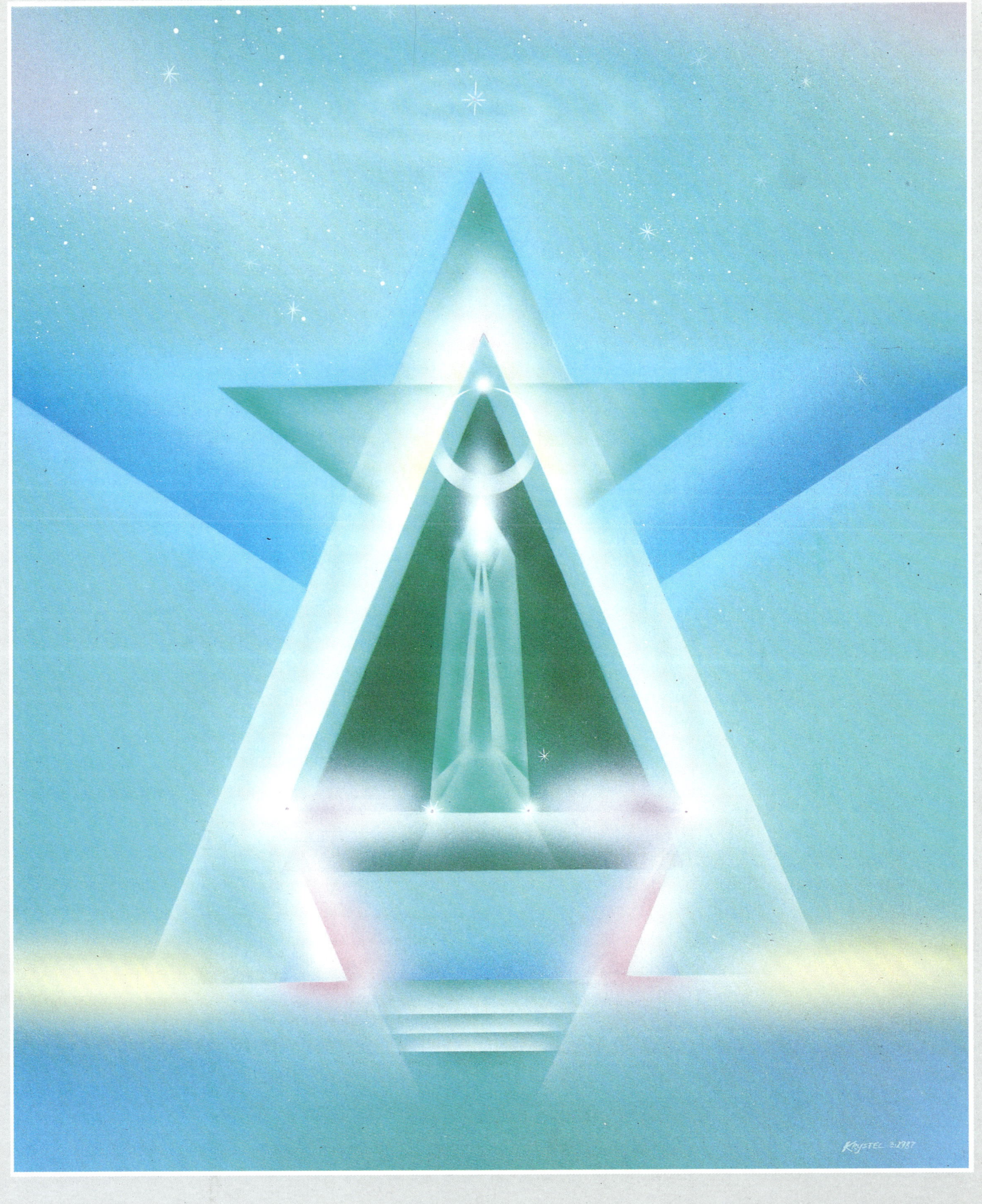
KRYSTEL

Lanikai
Krystel

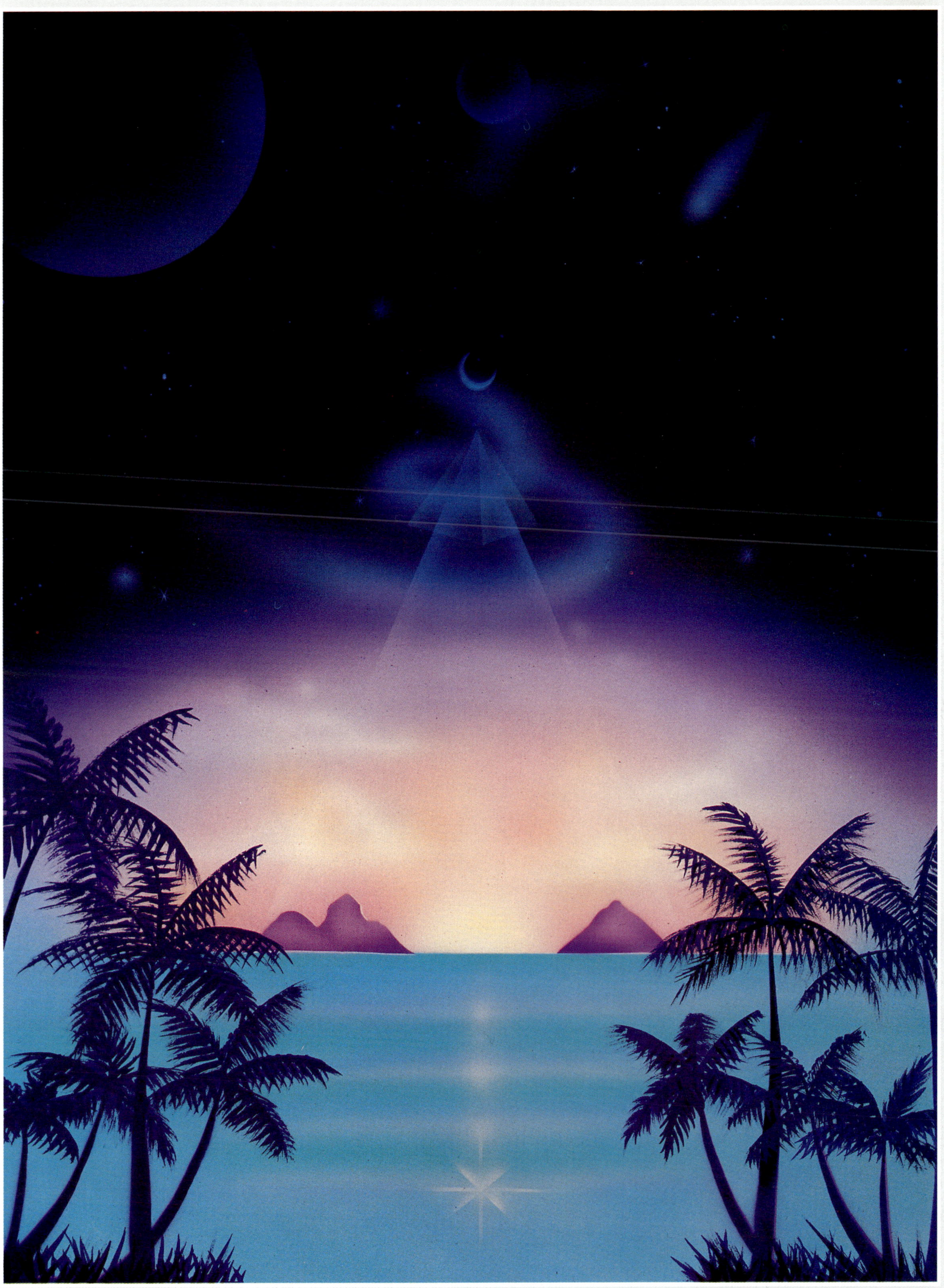

Iris
Krystel

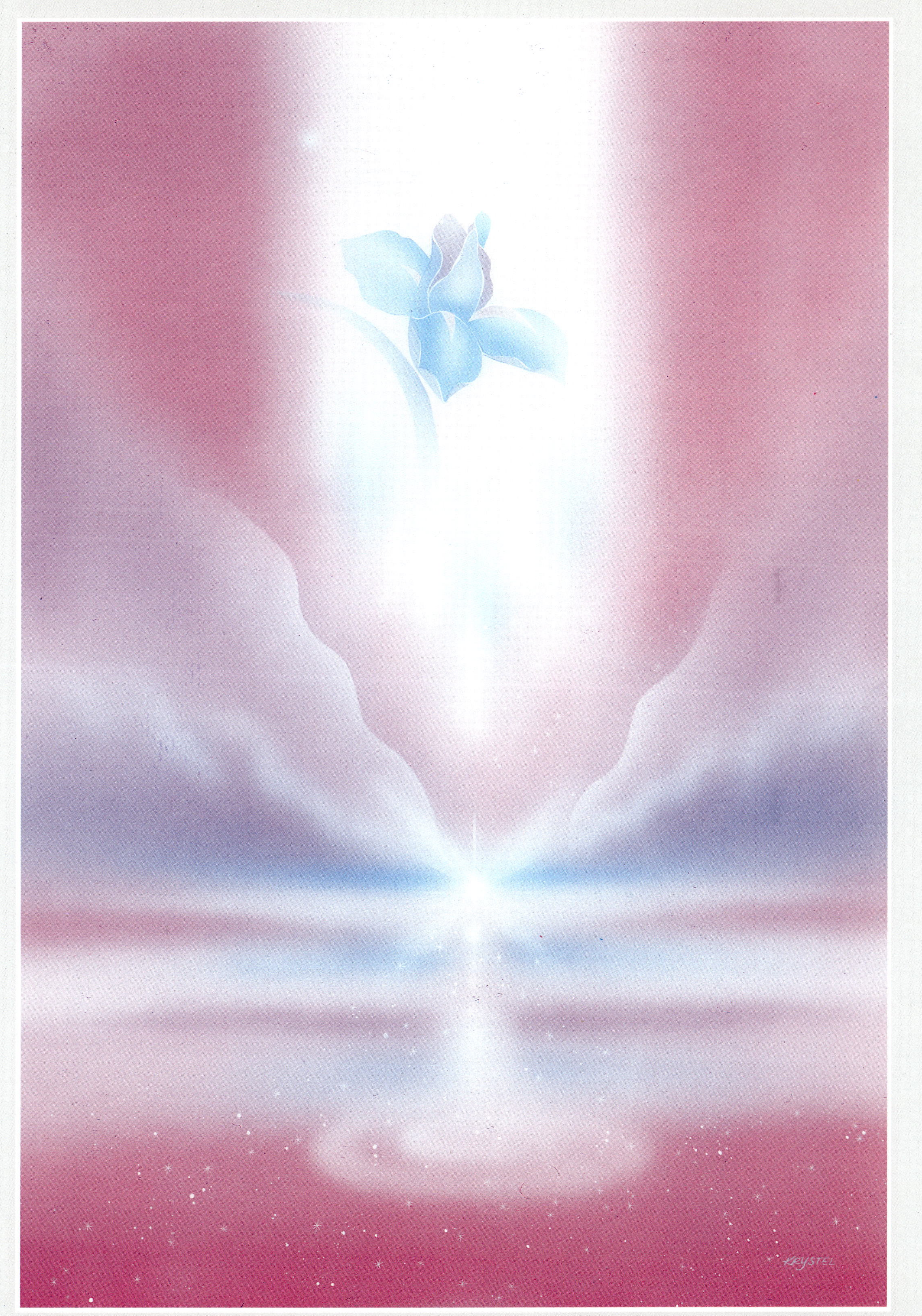
KRYSTEL

Nightsky
Krystel

Intimacy *(L)*
Krystel

Inner Light *(R)*
Krystel

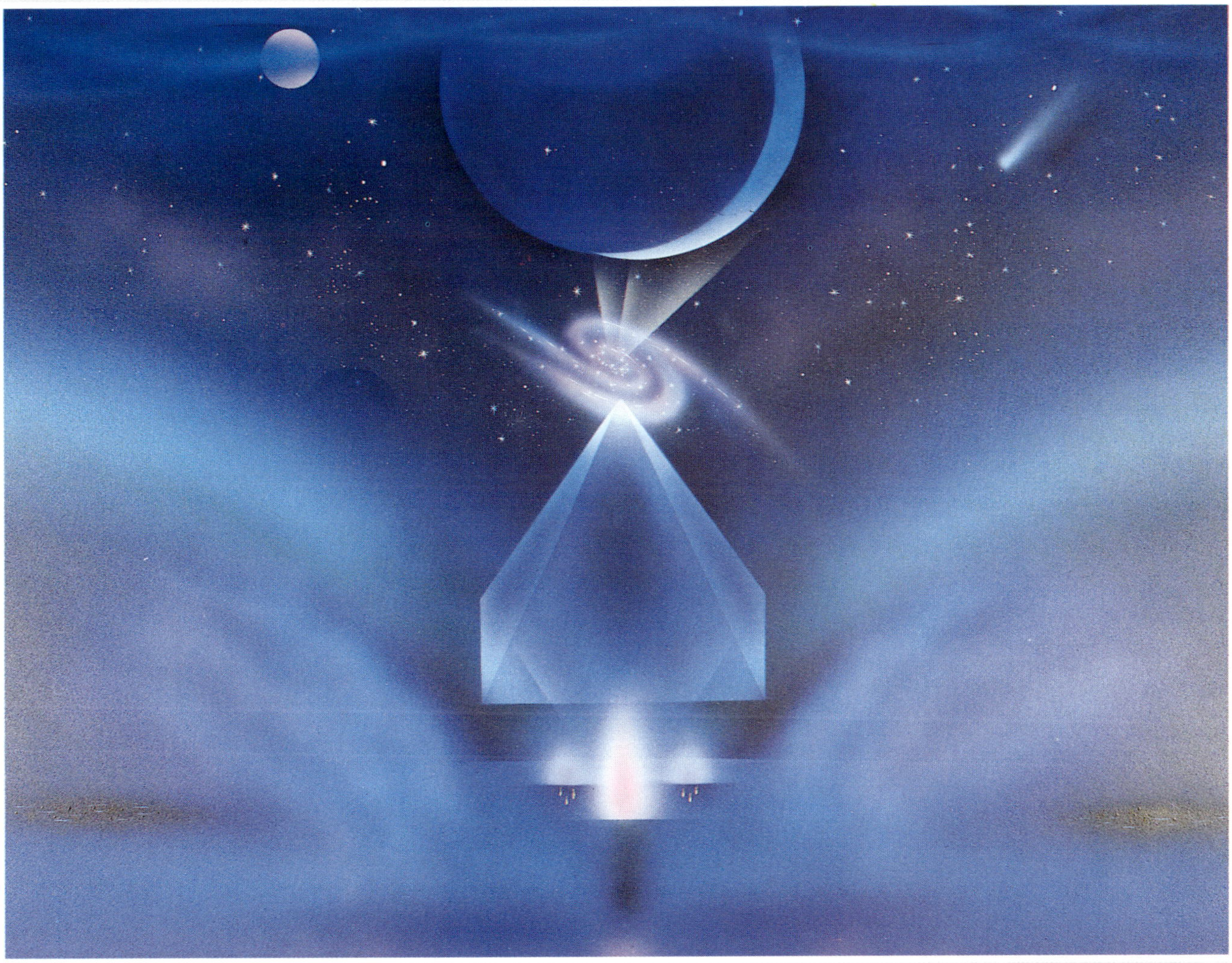

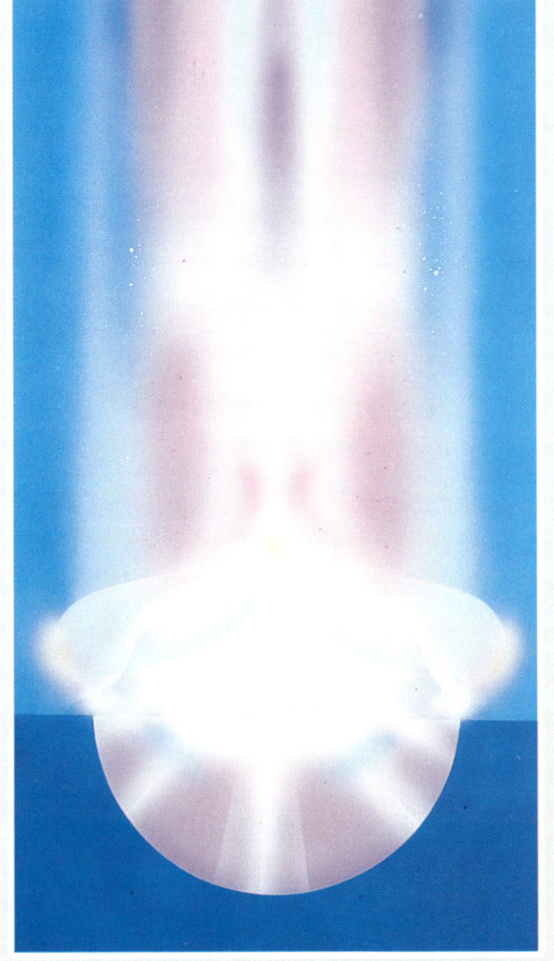
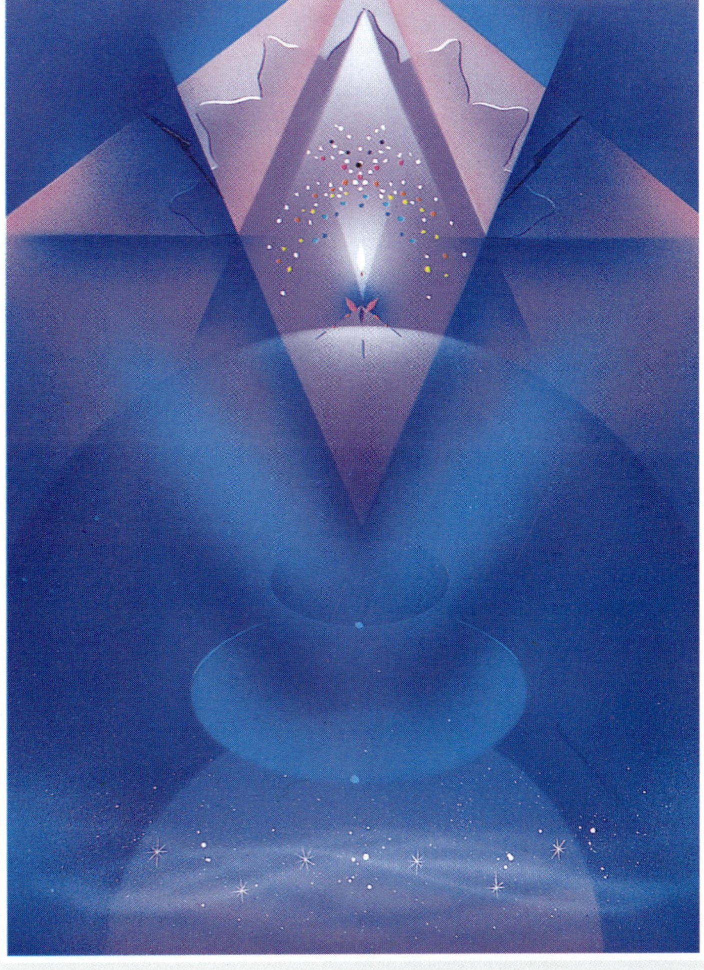

LEONARDO RENE

When an artist reaches into the depths of imagination searching for that unique subject of meaningful expression, the love for the work resonates through each finished creation. If you stare into a painting and it begins to draw you into the full impact of the artist's design, consider the well-crafted manipulations of pigment a direct viewpoint into the spirit of the painter.

Should an individual welcome the process of evolving from novice to adept in any given field, as part of life's character development, every aspect of the procedure becomes a significant part of the person's unique course of unfoldment toward a greater awareness.

"If our first love in art is to inspire humanity with our imagery, then the courage of our own convictions can become the motivation to approach art as a way of life, as well as a profession."

Portrait of an Artist

written by Rubin Zalez

copyright 1988

In 1981 a gifted young man of Native Mexican American heritage set aside his percussion instruments and commenced to single-pointedly teach himself to paint the visions of his mind. Less than three years later it became evident that Leonardo René Gonzalez was already making an impact in the California art world. Though still a novice with little recognition, a distinguished gallery of the San Francisco Bay Area requested the use of one of his images to be published as a large color postcard promoting the first major exhibit of his career.

Born December 9, 1958, Leonardo began his artistic lifestyle as a musician. By the time he was 17 years old he was touring the midwest with a popular

Detail of 24'' x 48''
Leonardo René

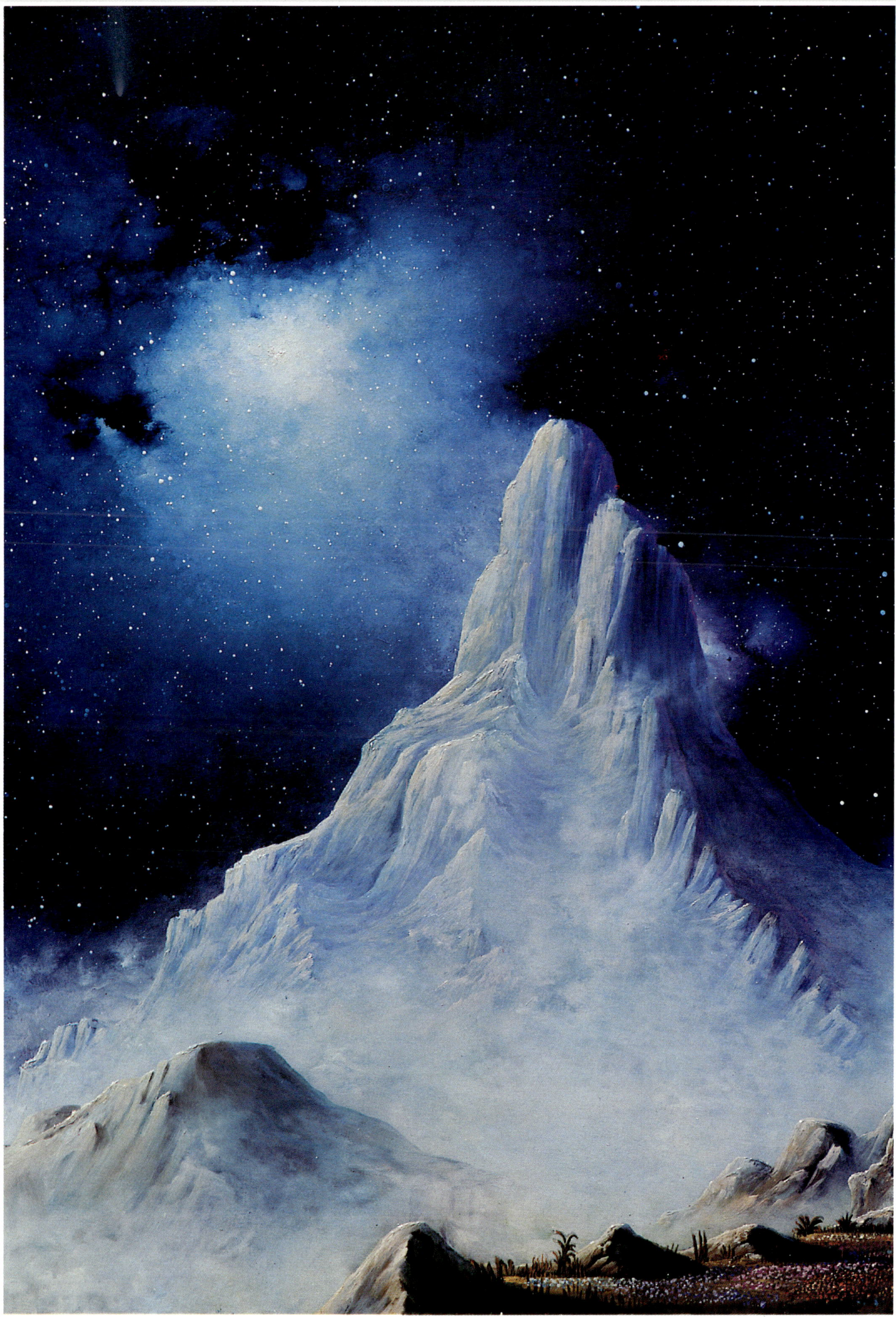

12 piece band. After moving to California where he continued to develop as a percussionist, the artist began to realize his growing desire for a more lasting expression than playing someone else's music. It was at this point that a friend asked Leonardo what he was contributing to inspire humanity. Unsatisfied with what he found to be his answer the artist began searching inside himself for the truth. Months later he began to notice how enjoyable drawing had become. As time progressed his passion and commitment for this new medium deepened. Inspired by vivid dreams and visions he experienced, Leonardo began to alter the direction of his creative development in ways that would take him years to begin understanding. In theory Leonardo's strategy to learn the art of oil painting was simple enough. Yet, the actuality of what the determined novice had set out to accomplish became a considerable task for any established painter, much less a musician who was changing courses in mid stream.

Although the subtle message and mood of Leonardo's visual work seems far removed from the hard driving Jazz and Afro-Cuban rhythms which dominate his musical passions. The same intense energy emanates through each painting. A discriminating balance of refined detail and brilliance cause the viewer's senses to still with satisfaction.

From the first glance Leonardo's paintings captivate and mystify you with striking three dimensional simulation that draws the eyes into the literal depth of each painting. His compositions depict the light and movement of shimmering nebula as they emit electric hues from a distance far beneath the orbiting planets of other solar systems. The sense of an endless universe is captured within the confines of the canvas.

Detail of 18'' x 24''
Leonardo René

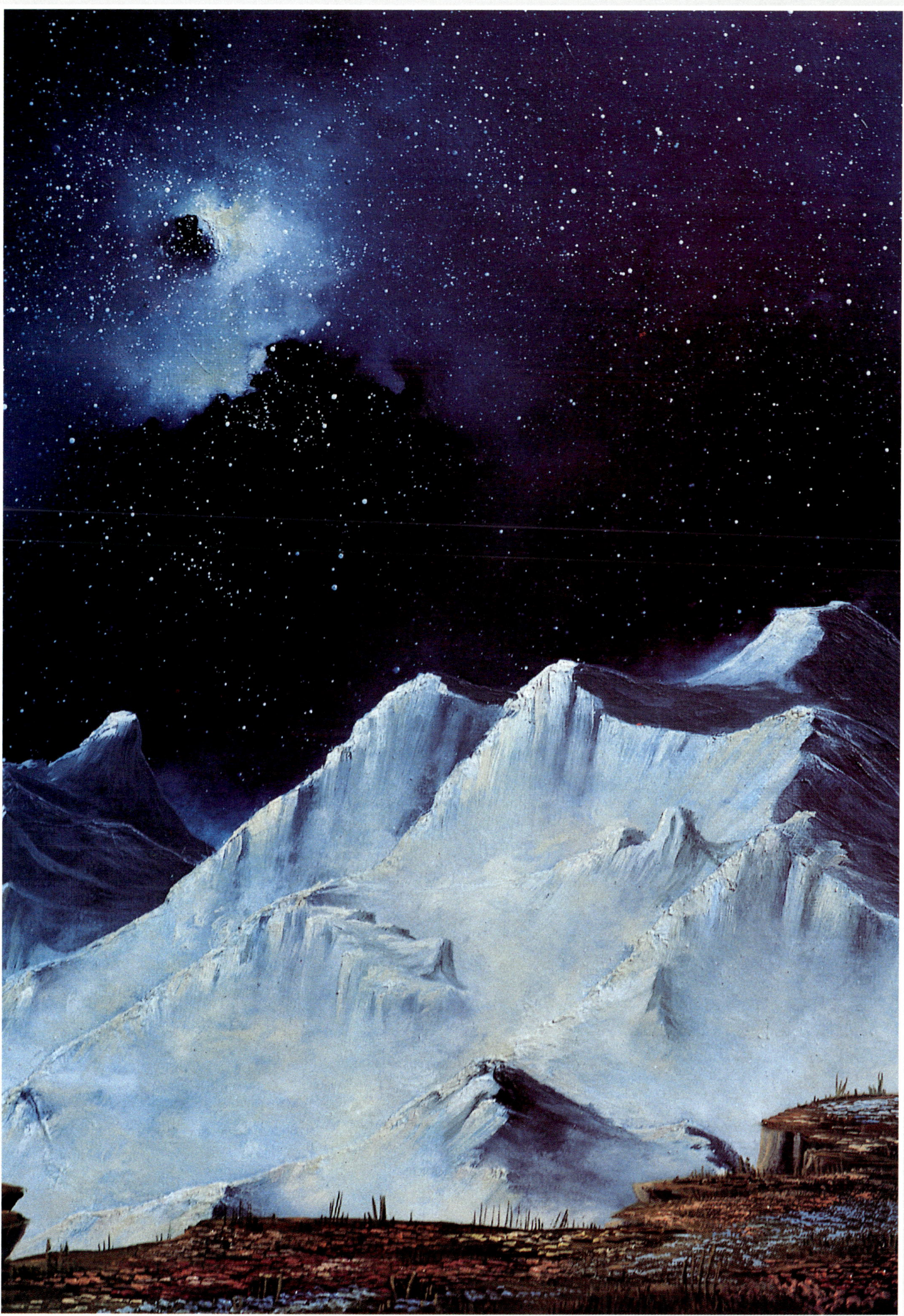

This mesmerizing effect of deep space is the result of the artist's commitment to introduce an innovative direction in oil painting. Through the use of his specialized design in bristle and sable brushes the artist has perfected the methodical procedures that create the imagery which has characterized his unique style. By capturing the actual depth of luminosity within the universe, Leonardo's work has reached beyond the present limits of Space-Art realism. With an imaginative eye for beauty both sublime and sensual, the artist portrays the astronomical phenomenon which is literally the womb of all physical life.

Detail of Deep Space
Leonardo René

Detail of Deep Space
Leonardo René

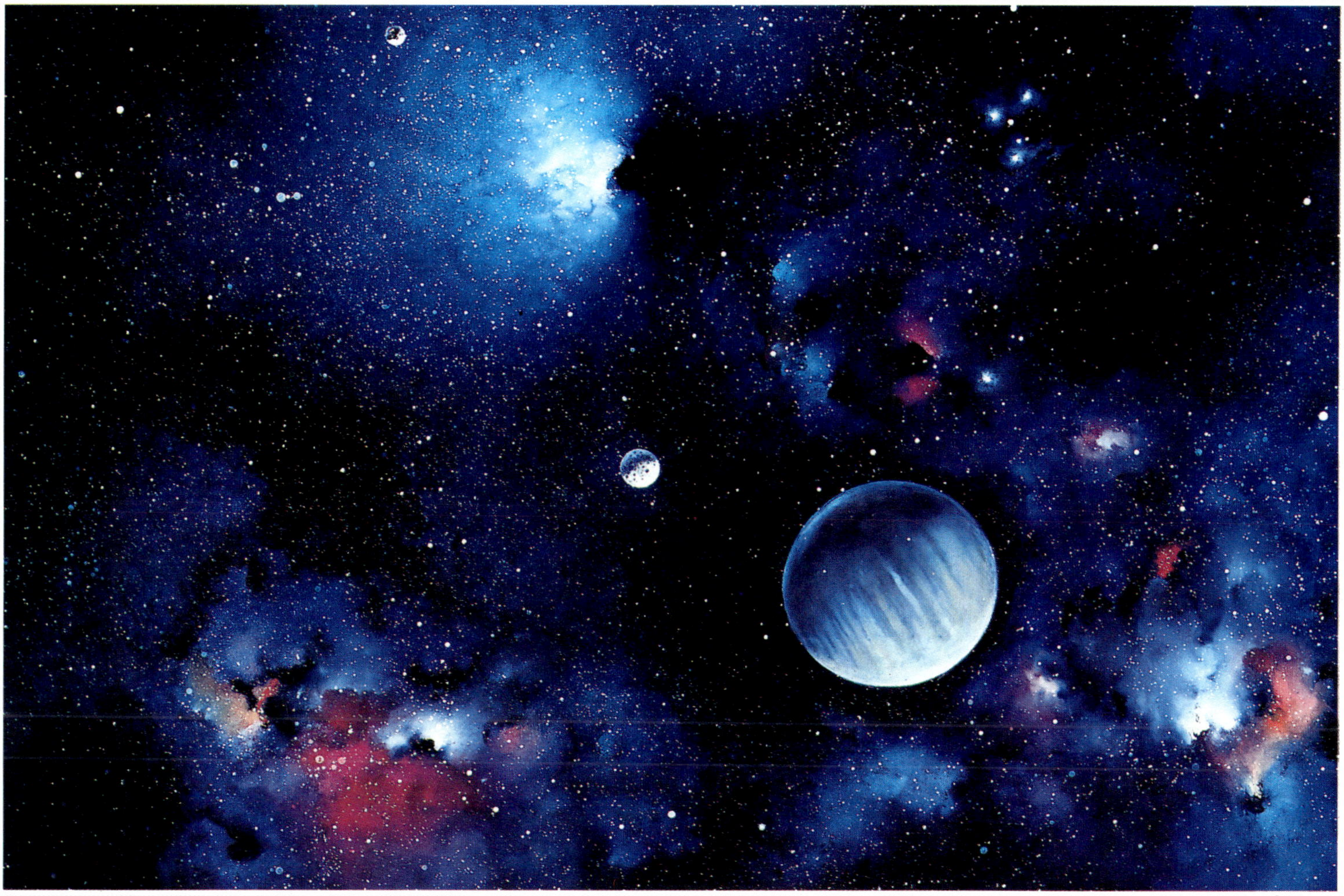

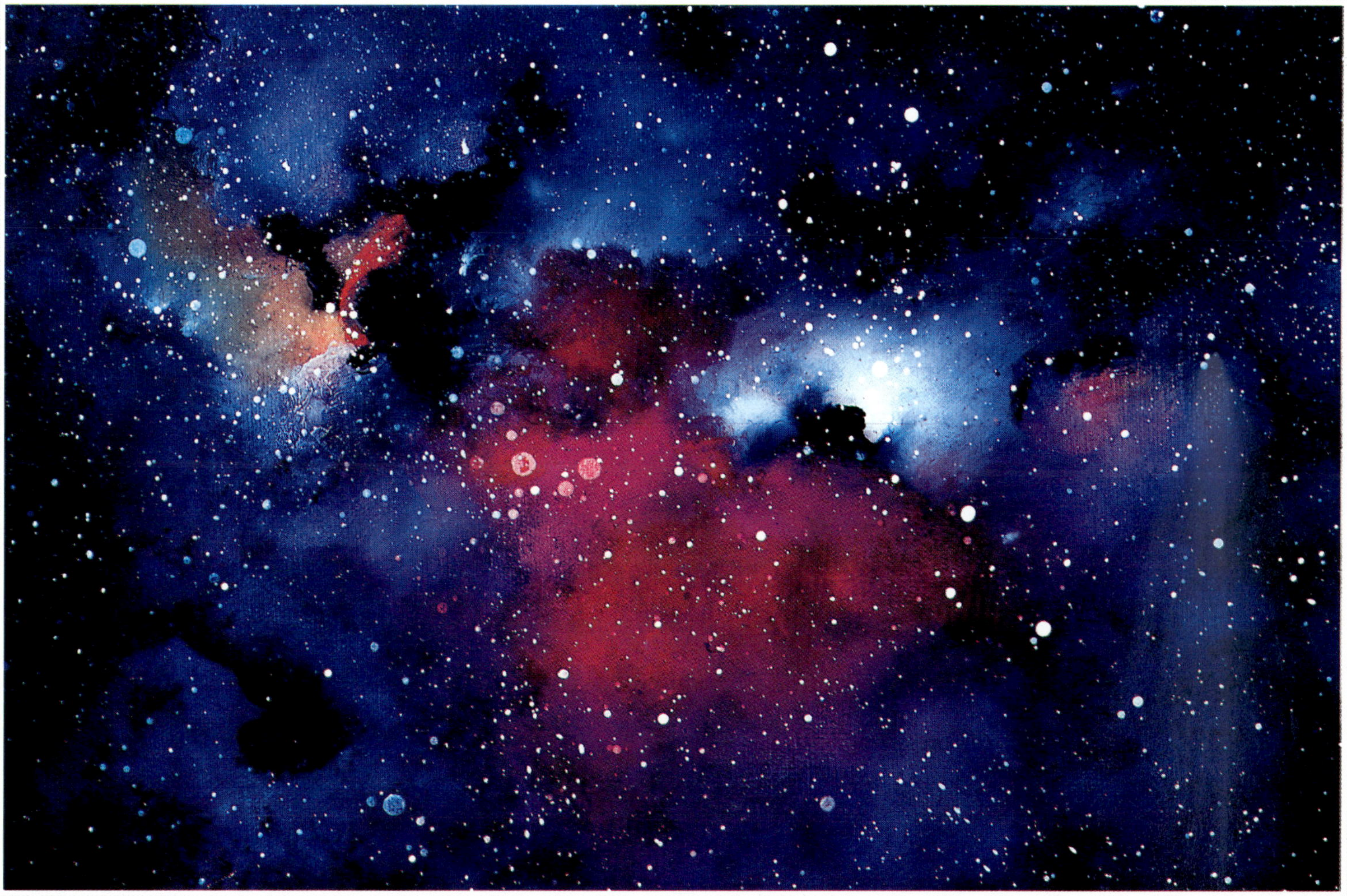

Detail of Intervention
Leonardo René

Detail of Untitled
Leonardo René

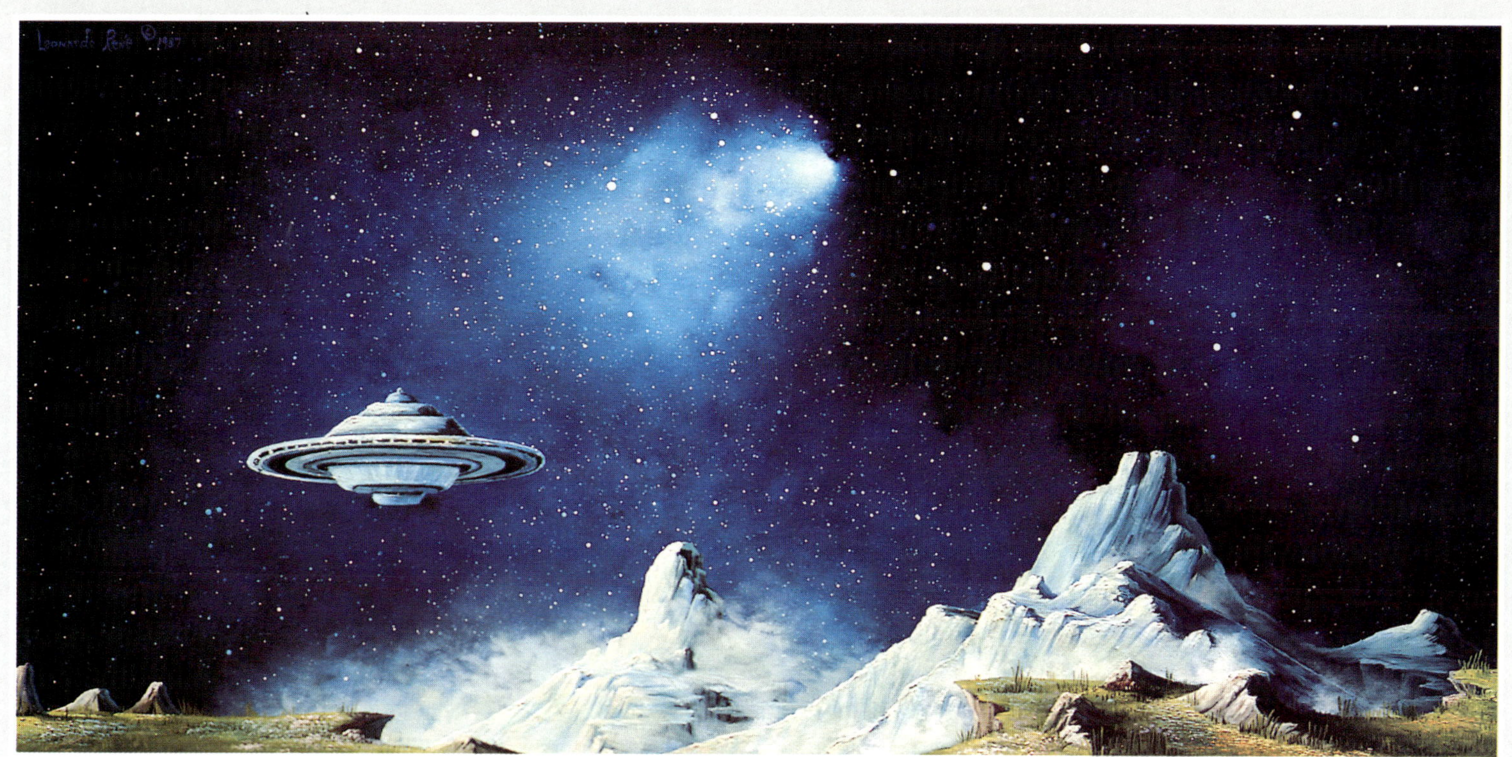

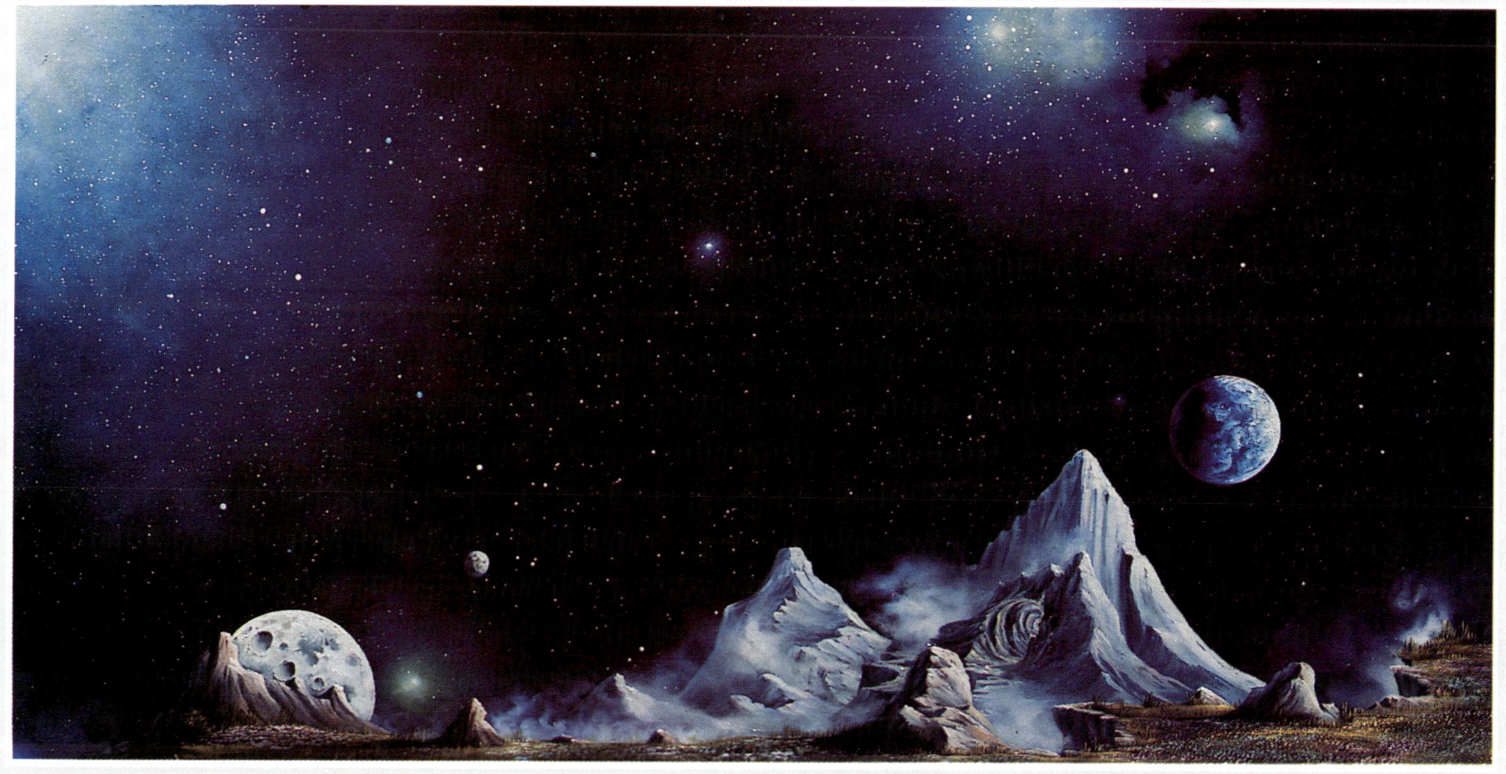

RODNEY BIRKETT

Rodney Birkett, native of San Francisco, Virgo extraodinaire. Arts and Crafts ran strongly through the family even though the real call to paint came later in life.

Music was a strong influence to the young Rodney. He majored in music throughout High School in which he achieved a degree.

After a very diversified life which included photography, lithography, graphic design and commercial art, he decided to turn to the Fine Arts. Being influenced by the infamous Salvador Dali, and the surrealistic movement, living in true Bohemian style in the early San Francisco Beat Generation of North Beach, he formed his styles and early visions. Having no formal education in the arts and mainly self taught, he met and formed a friendship with George Summner, a Bay Area environmental painter, who brought him to a new level of artistic expression. In the early 80s, he moved to Mt. Shasta and became exposed to the mystical and inner teachings of the Self. This brought about a new level of understanding and awareness that he could now translate into what is now known as "Visionary Art."

Combining surrealism, fantasy and a very meticulous, highly develped and polished technique, he achieves a new dimension of imagery. Using nature and his own mystical experiences and inspiration he is able to realize on canvas new and exciting creations.

Heaven on Earth
Rodney Birkett

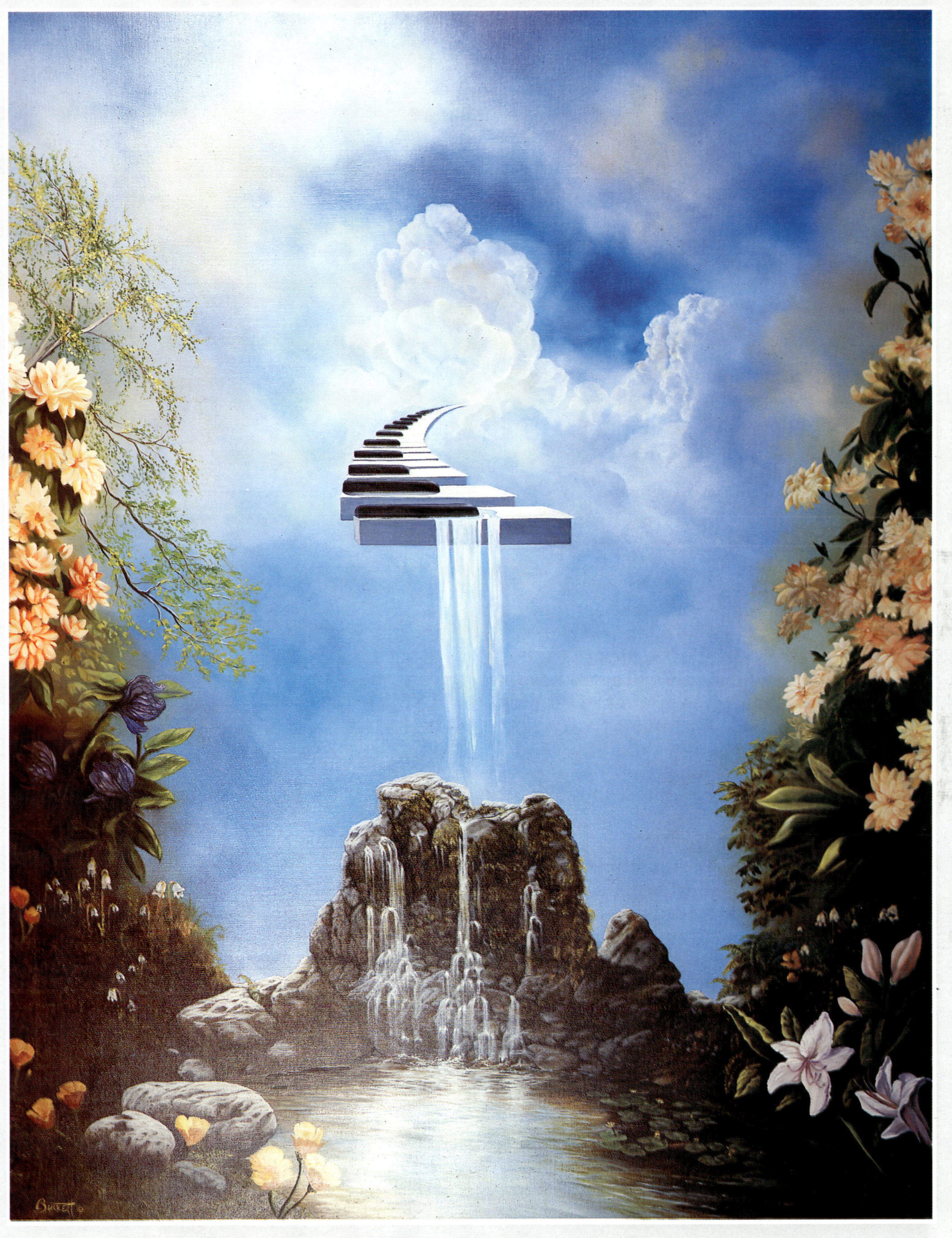

Rodney Birkett— Man of Mystery

by Jeffrey Palmer

As it happened, my first meeting with Rodney occurred one crystaline evening at the opening of a showing in a prestigious downtown second-story gallery. He was sitting on a white upholstered bolster, glass of wine in hand. Overhead tracks lit the stark twelve foot walls illuminating paintings which looked like doorways into other worlds. Against the highly polished oak floors the illusion became more vivid, compelling me toward the largest of a group of four facing the entryway. Stopping six feet from its center I knew I had seen this place before. Logically no place on Earth could so appear. I couldn't move being drawn deeper into a reality I knew; and missed terribly.

I didn't want to leave. This was more than the art I had come to expect, it felt like a way to be. When finished Rodney was still sitting, now talking to an attractive woman in her thirties. As I approached she turned and walked away and without intention I was introducing myself to this man who had created such a longing in my heart. His smile was deep and as he got up to shake hands I realized the power in his presence. His face was chiseled by what looked like deep space, his eyes transparent. I found myself asking something trite like where do you live, he answered with a laugh. I liked him instantly.

As we talked I came to know a being who seemed to be everywhere. Preferring the extremes of nature, often alone; he had no home I could discern, his life occupied by mysterious journeys to magical places. His stories of desert, jungle and mountain were intimately linked to his art. The accounts were those of a space voyager describing the

Crystal Starburst
Rodney Birkett

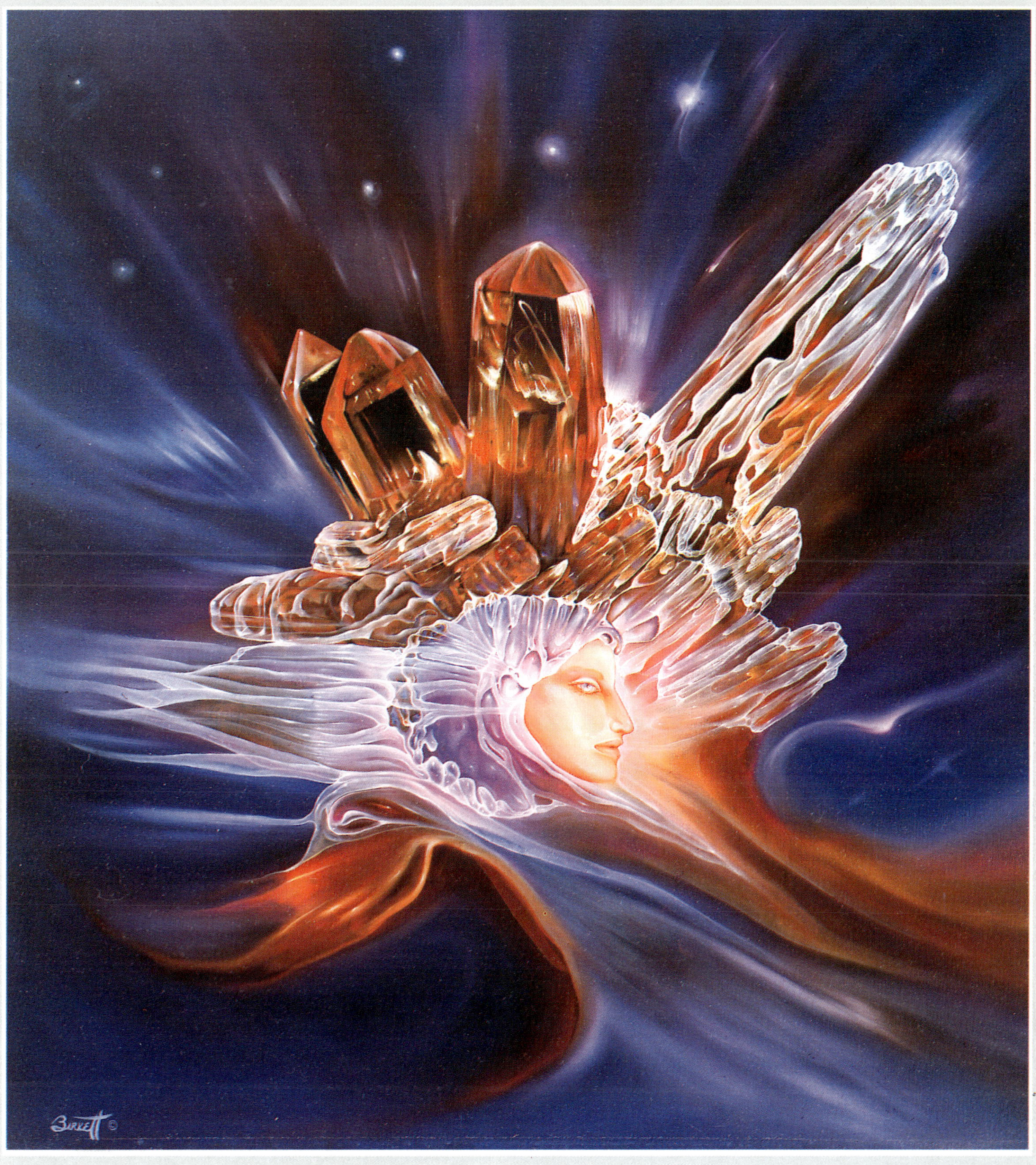

delights of the galaxy. I was fascinated and began to feel at home wanting to live in this world beyond. His works are windows into other dimensions. He explained, "It is my intent to provide the viewer with a sense of peace that gives understanding and the feeling of being transported into one's own consciousness of the eternal."

Eternal it was. Hours had passed and the time had come to say our goodbye's and go out into the night. I felt as though I was waking from a special dream, but under my arm was a painting, a link through which I could always return.

The Mysteries of
the Crystal Skull Revealed
Rodney Birkett

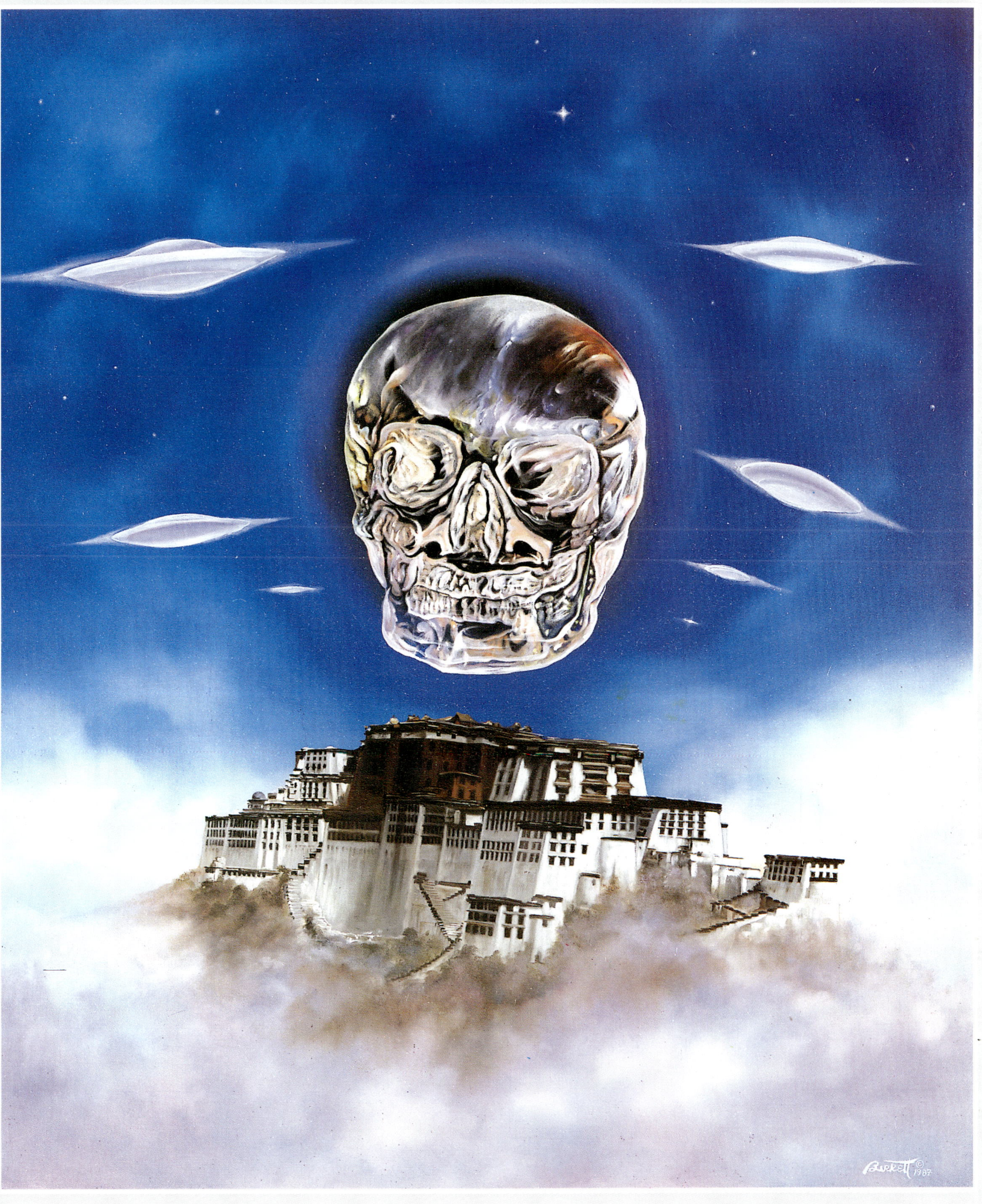
© 1987

Maganda
Rodney Birkett

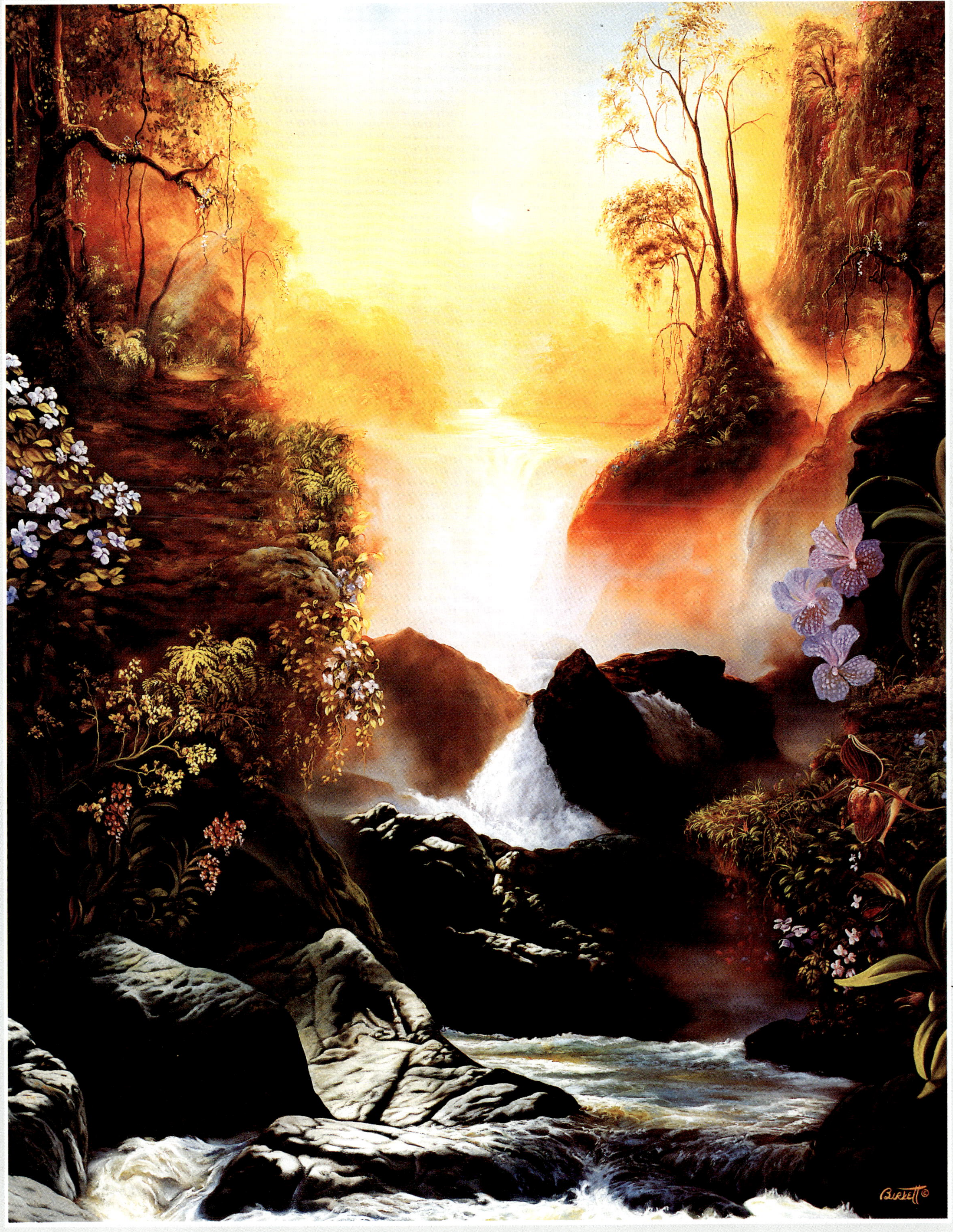
BURKETT©

The Opalescent Dragon
Rodney Birkett

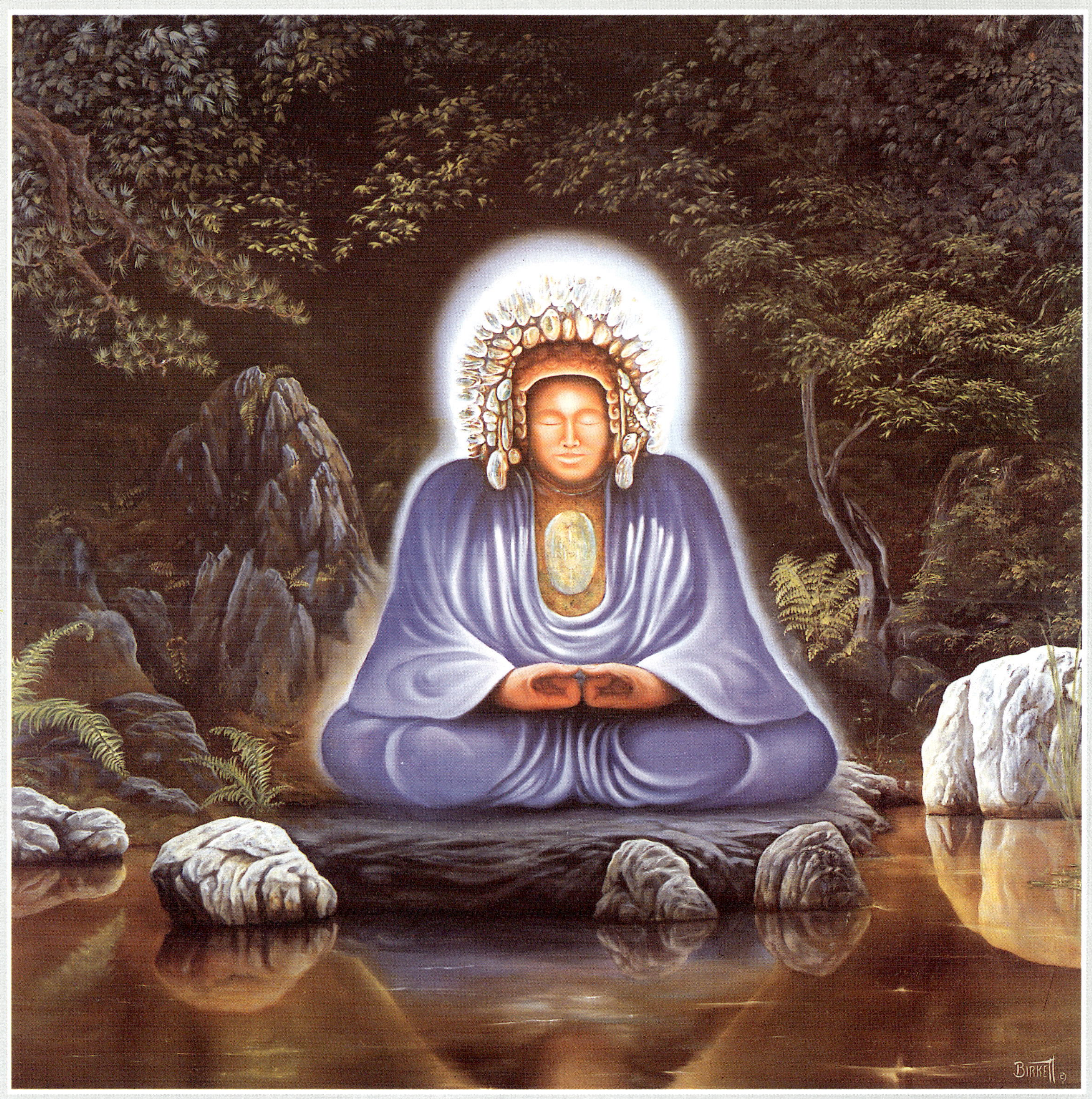
BIRKETT

The Saturn Arches
Rodney Birkett

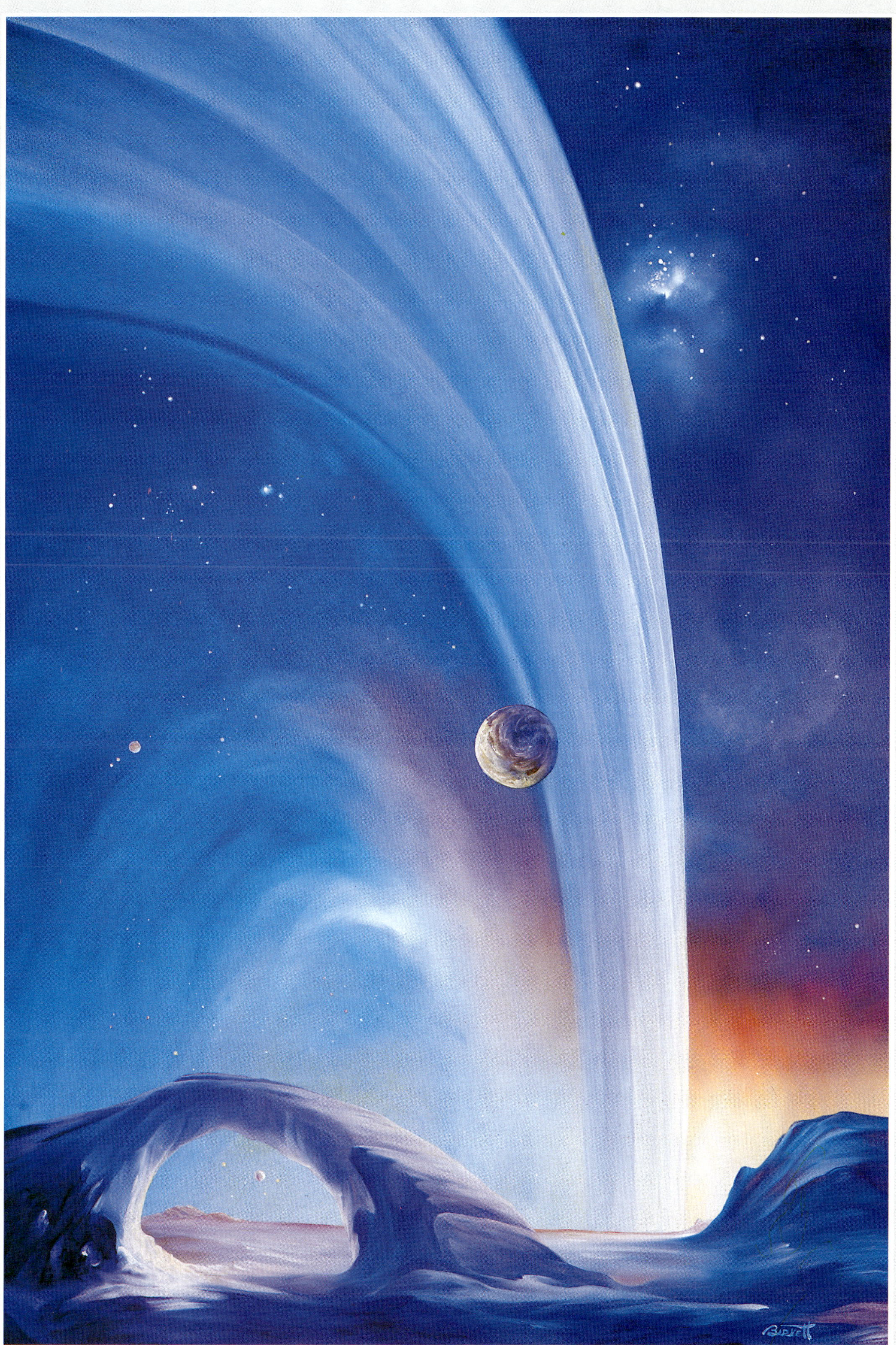

Mt. Shasta Goddess
Rodney Birkett

Solitude
Rodney Birkett

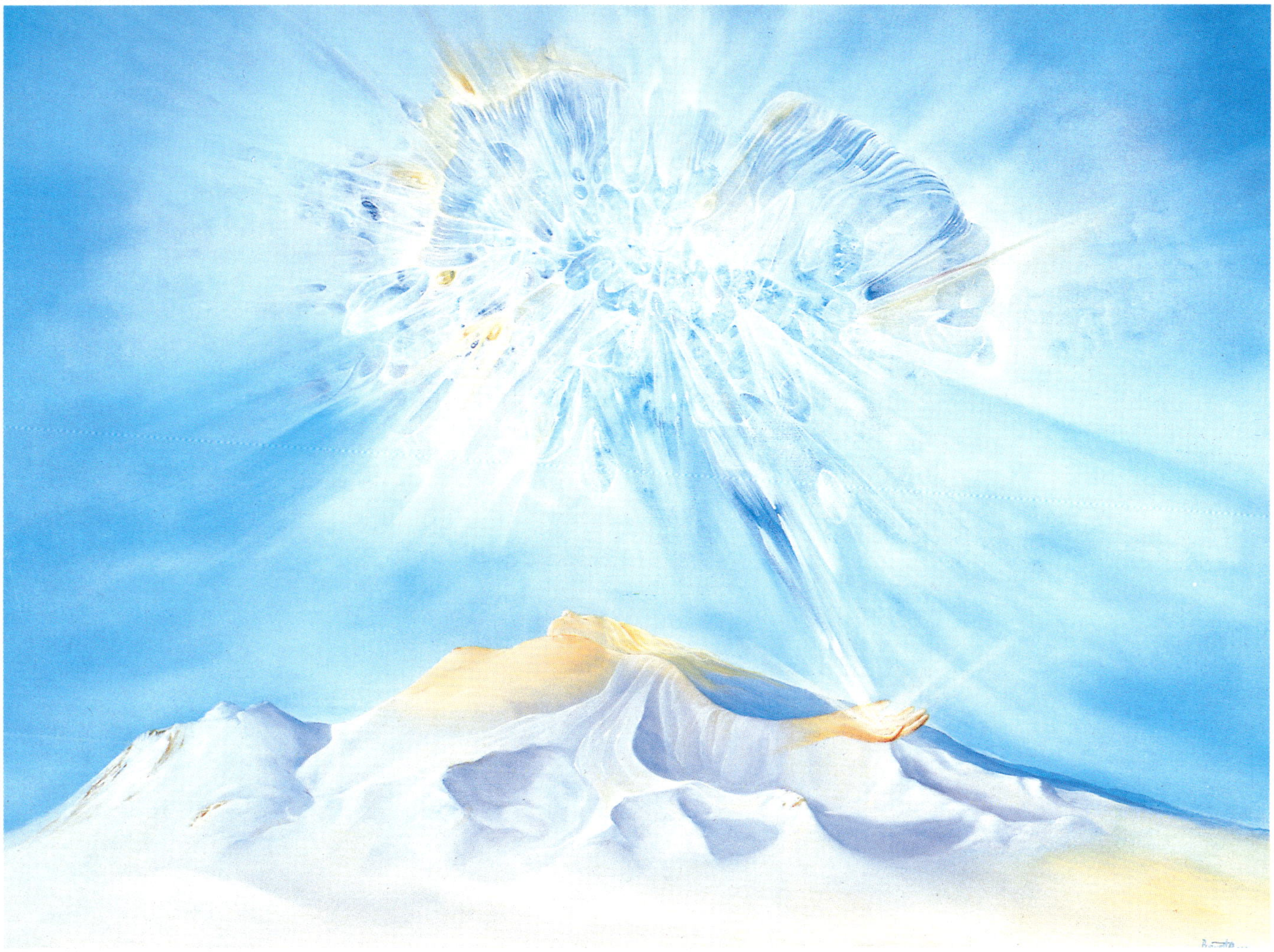

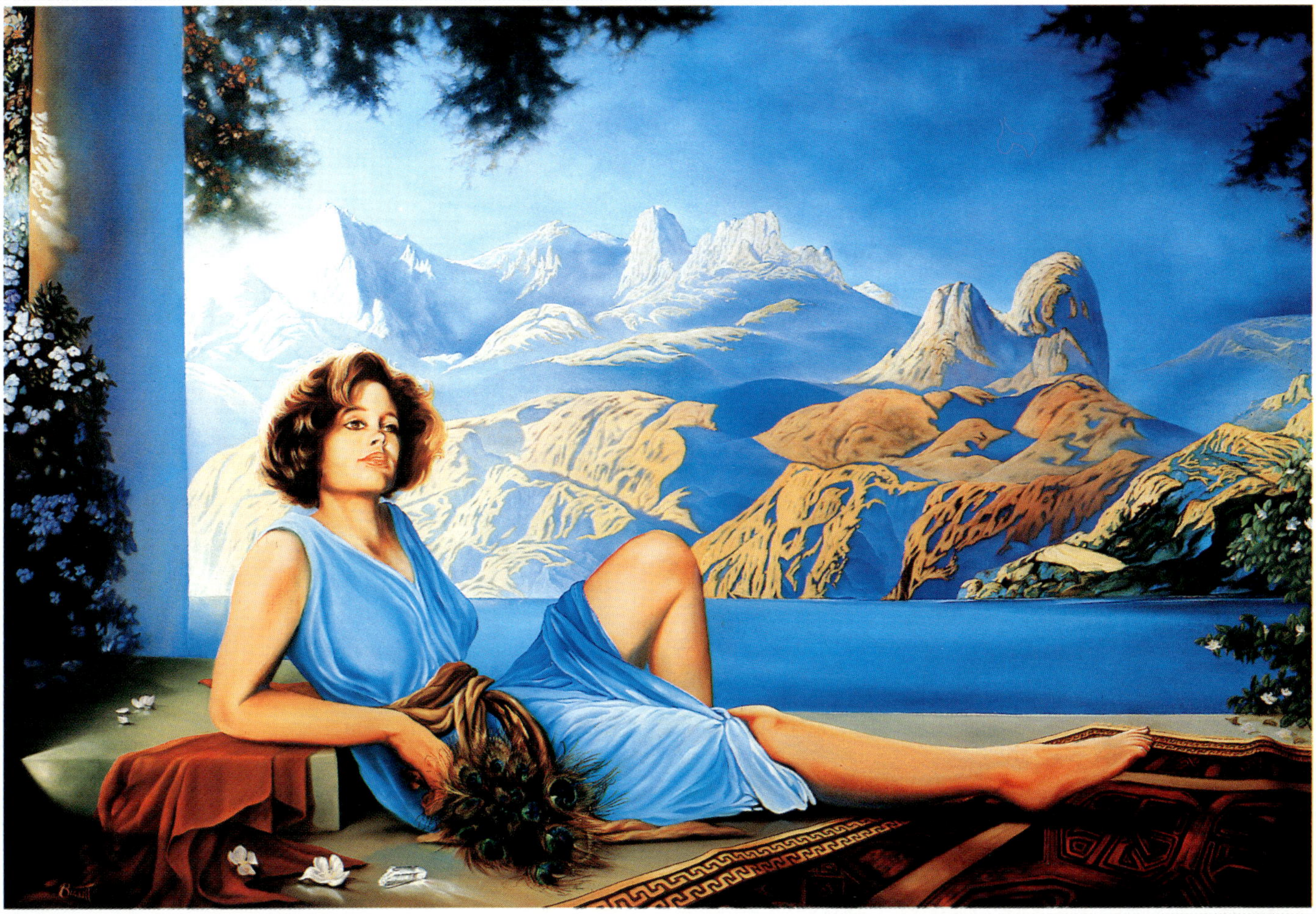

Time in Space
Rodney Birkett

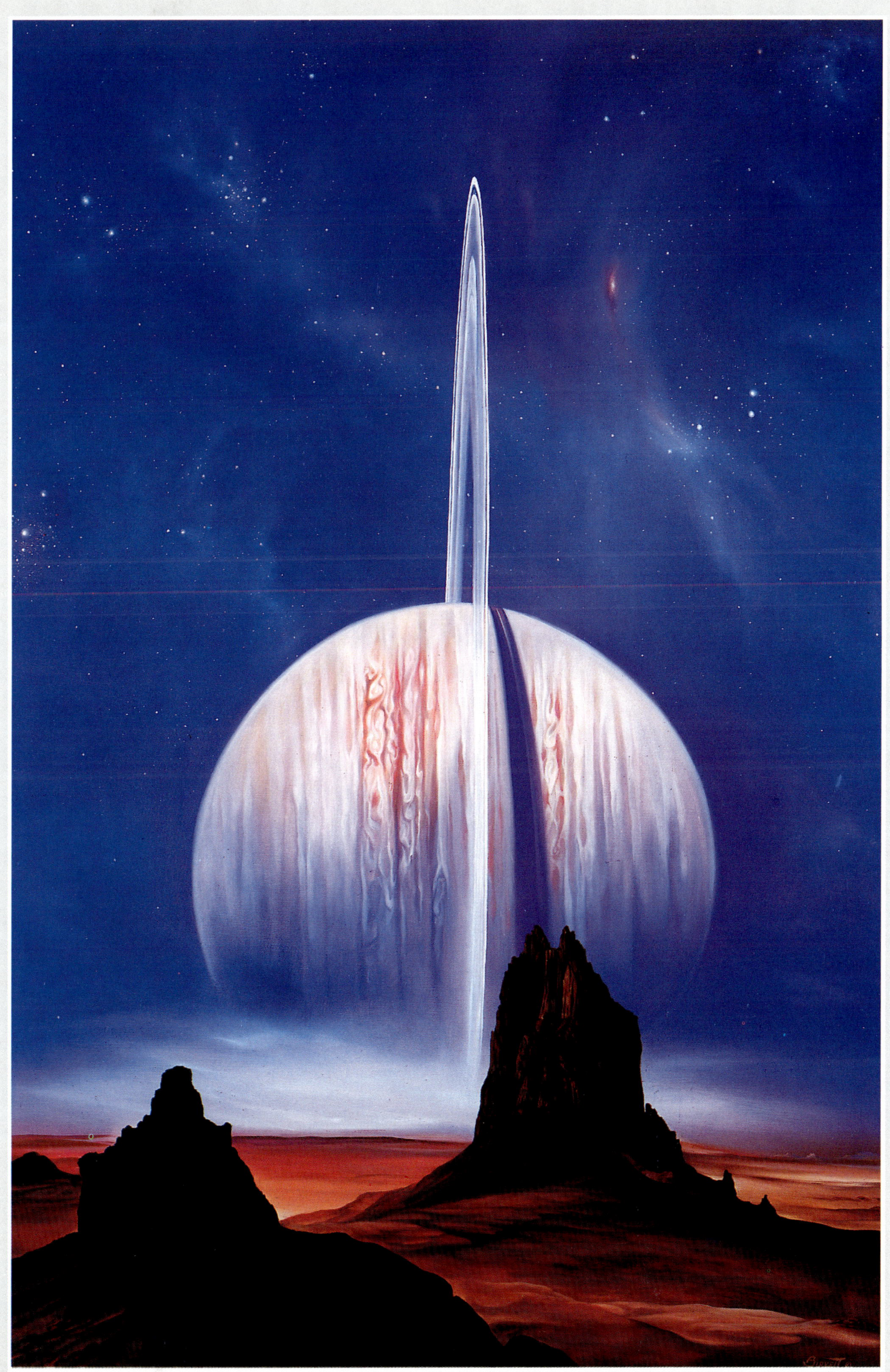

Crystal Lake
Rodney Birkett

Shambala
Rodney Birkett

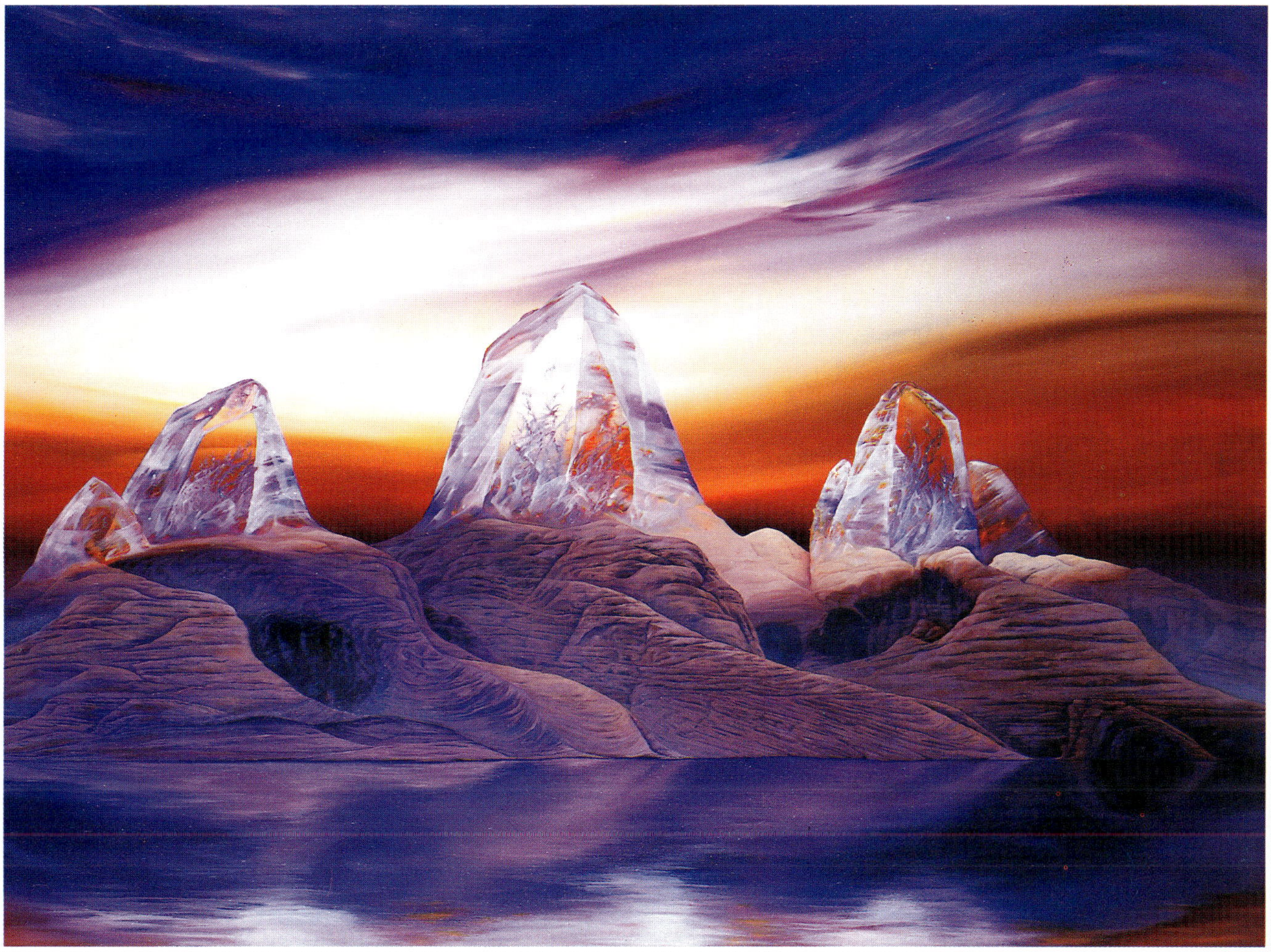

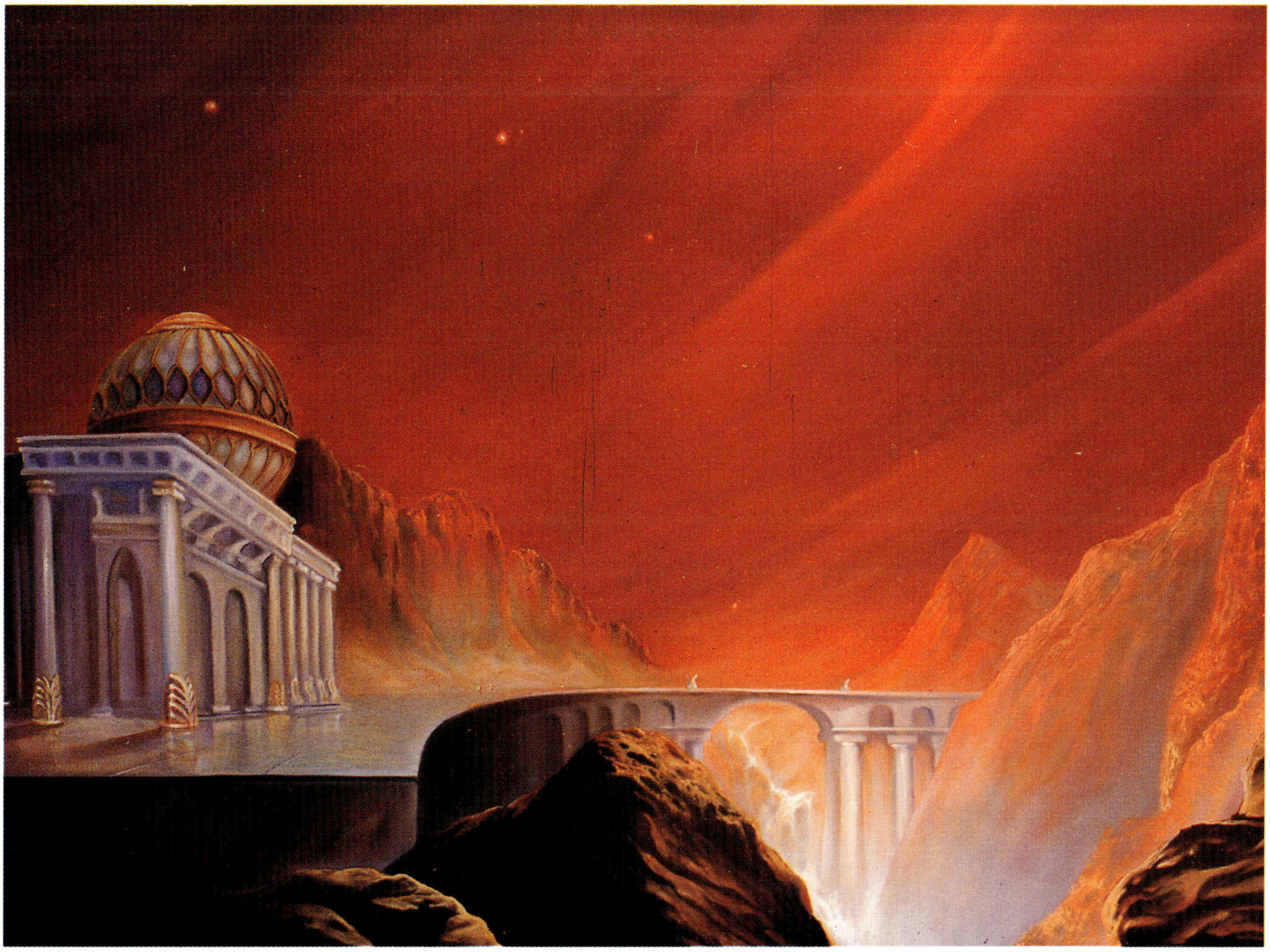

Dreams of Ecstasy
Rodney Birkett

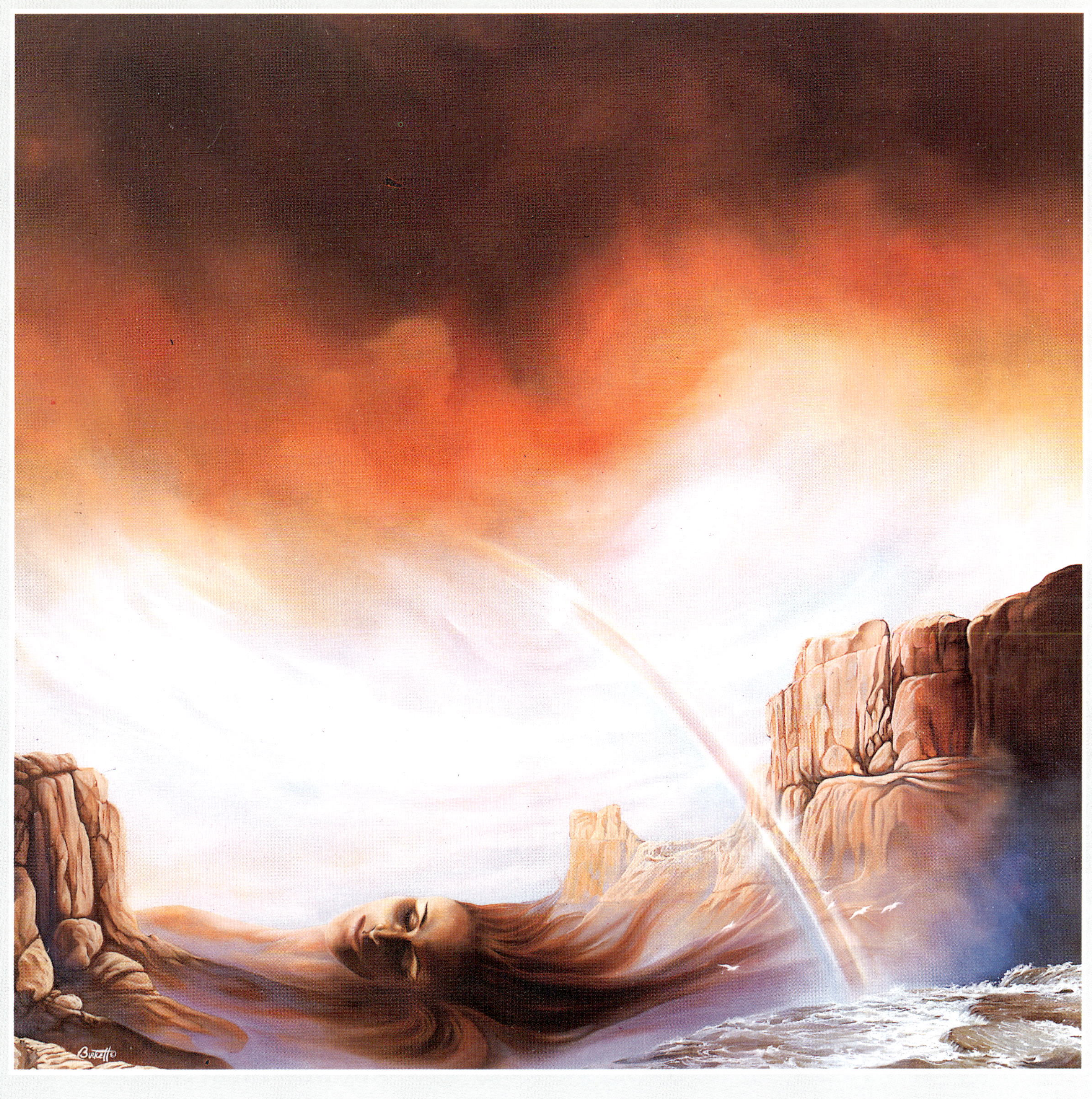

Amber Sunset
in Monument Valley
Rodney Birkett

Lightning Strikes
Rodney Birkett

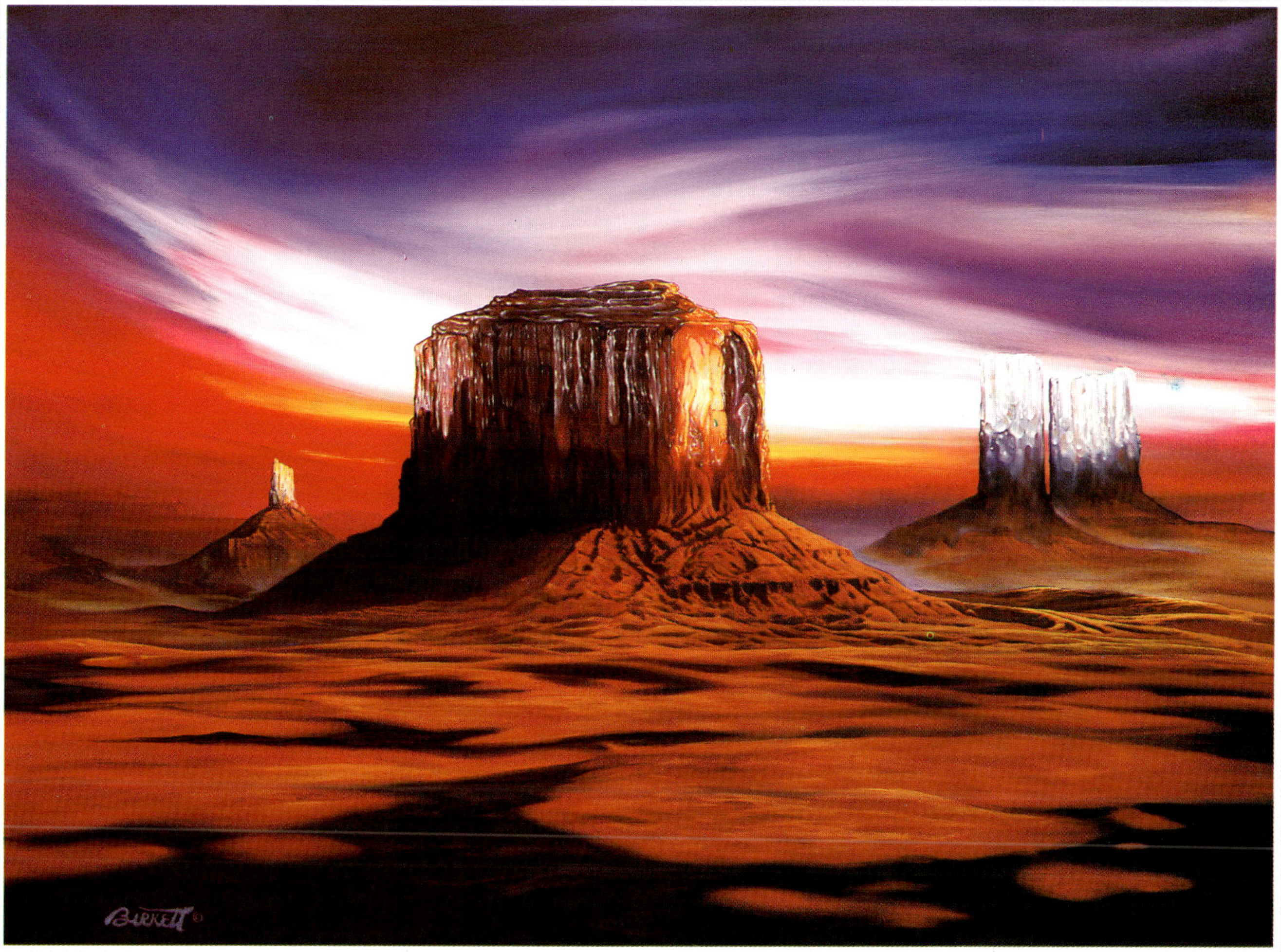

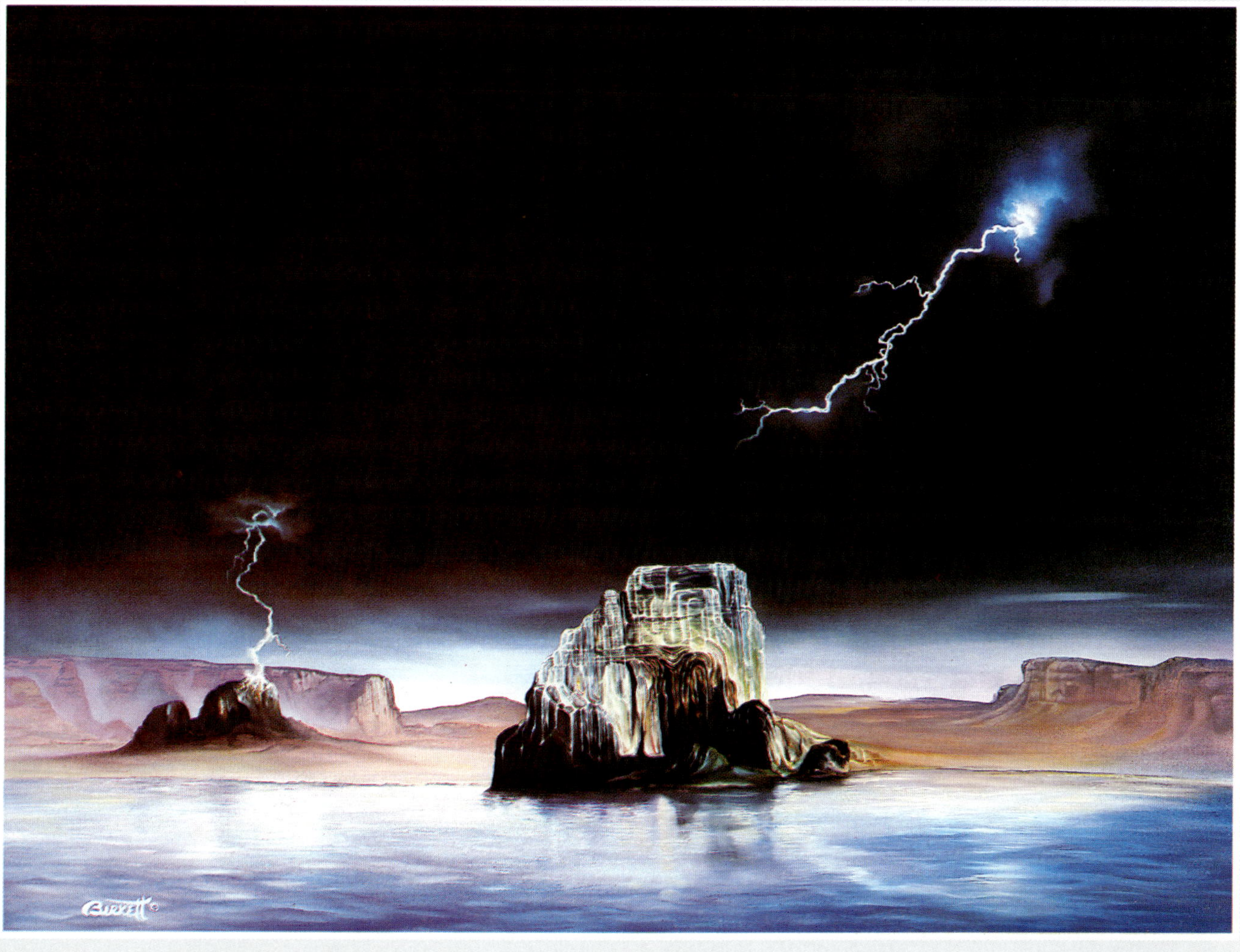

ANDRALERIA

ANDRALERIA—Andreé R. Oreck was born on Easter Sunday in Prague, Czechoslovakia. She spent her childhood in Paris, France and her teens commuting between Paris and New York. From the time she was eight years old, she knew she would be an artist—little knowing it would take almost a half a century to realize this conviction.

Her academic education, from the very start, was very erratic on the formal side and incredibly full and rich on the practical side. Her father, an international industrialist, took her on many of his travels through Europe. The family was multi-lingual and there never was less than three languages spoken at the dinner table. She started art school at the age of fifteen, going to La Grande Chaumiere and taking private lessons.

She came to California early in life and pursued her art by realizing she was unhappy doing anything else. She went to work for the animation industry and even though the pay then was poor at first, the glory of it was great. After nine years of working for CBS, Walt Disney, Warner Bros., etc., she became a free lance studio artist. At the same time, she continued her struggle to paint, draw and break into the fine arts world in Los Angeles.

In 1964, and three husbands later, she was finally given a major show and began to have small reviews in the *Los Angeles Times,* when the totally unforeseen happened and at 36 she became a mother and the studio became a nursery.

In 1966, she began to get involved in the raising and changing of her consciousness, which took a radical turn and caused a trip to India and Japan. From then on, the mystical side of her nature opened up and permanently altered her life.

In 1971, she moved to Mt. Shasta, California and published and illustrated a small series of some of her work.

The Master Seed
Andraleria

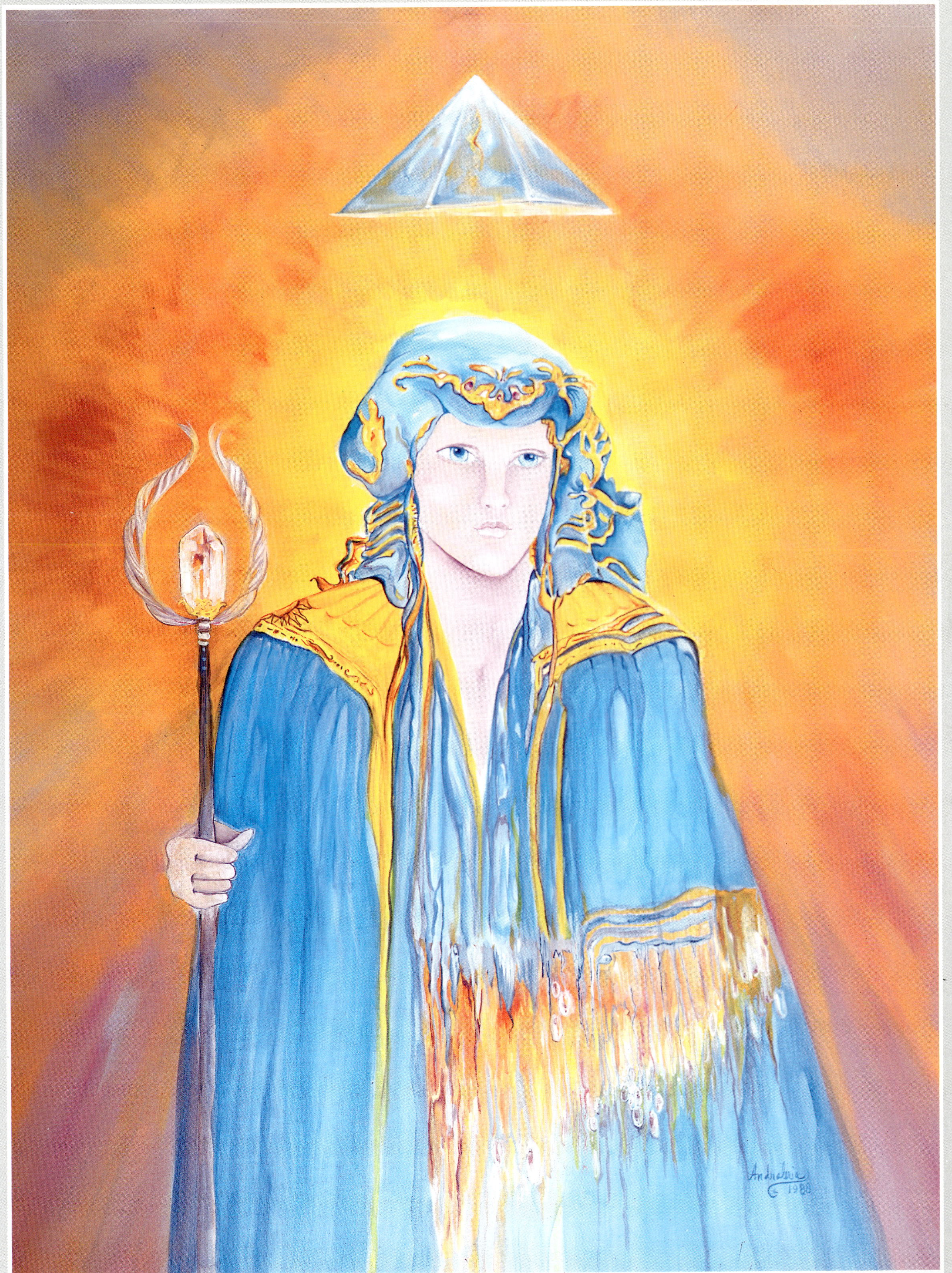

In 1977, she started painting again, she studied for a year with a self-taught artist, a great intuitive painter Rodney Birkett and for 1½ years she went to C.O.S., she studied with Bob Nugent. Mostly, however, she is self-taught, using a vast reference library of art of every kind.

She started showing at Blue Star Gallery in Ashland, Oregon in 1979, one of the few galleries that specialize in the Visionary and Fantastic type of art. After 5 years of exploring this very new and exciting art, she began her Discovery series.

In 1981, she designed an Astrological calendar called Celestial Influences for Quicksilver productions, which was published nationally that year.

"Art is a soul's expression, it is one of the ways to explore inner space, to capture the experience and reveal it on canvas. I hope to enrich all those who see my paintings. And through the magic of subjective communication to somewhat brighten their world."

Joyful Playmates
Andraleria

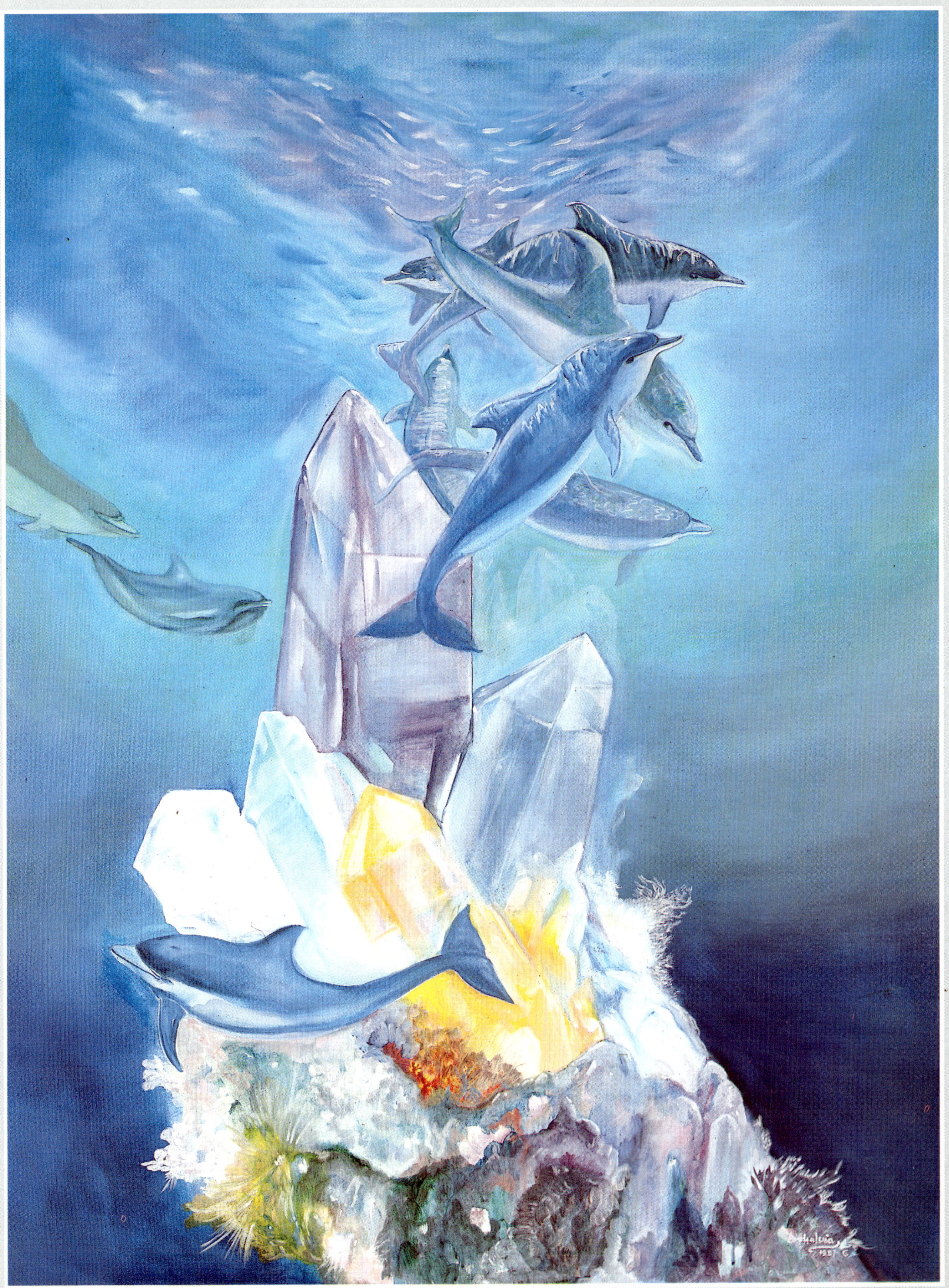

Atlantian Treasures
Andraleria

Gift of the Sea
Andraleria

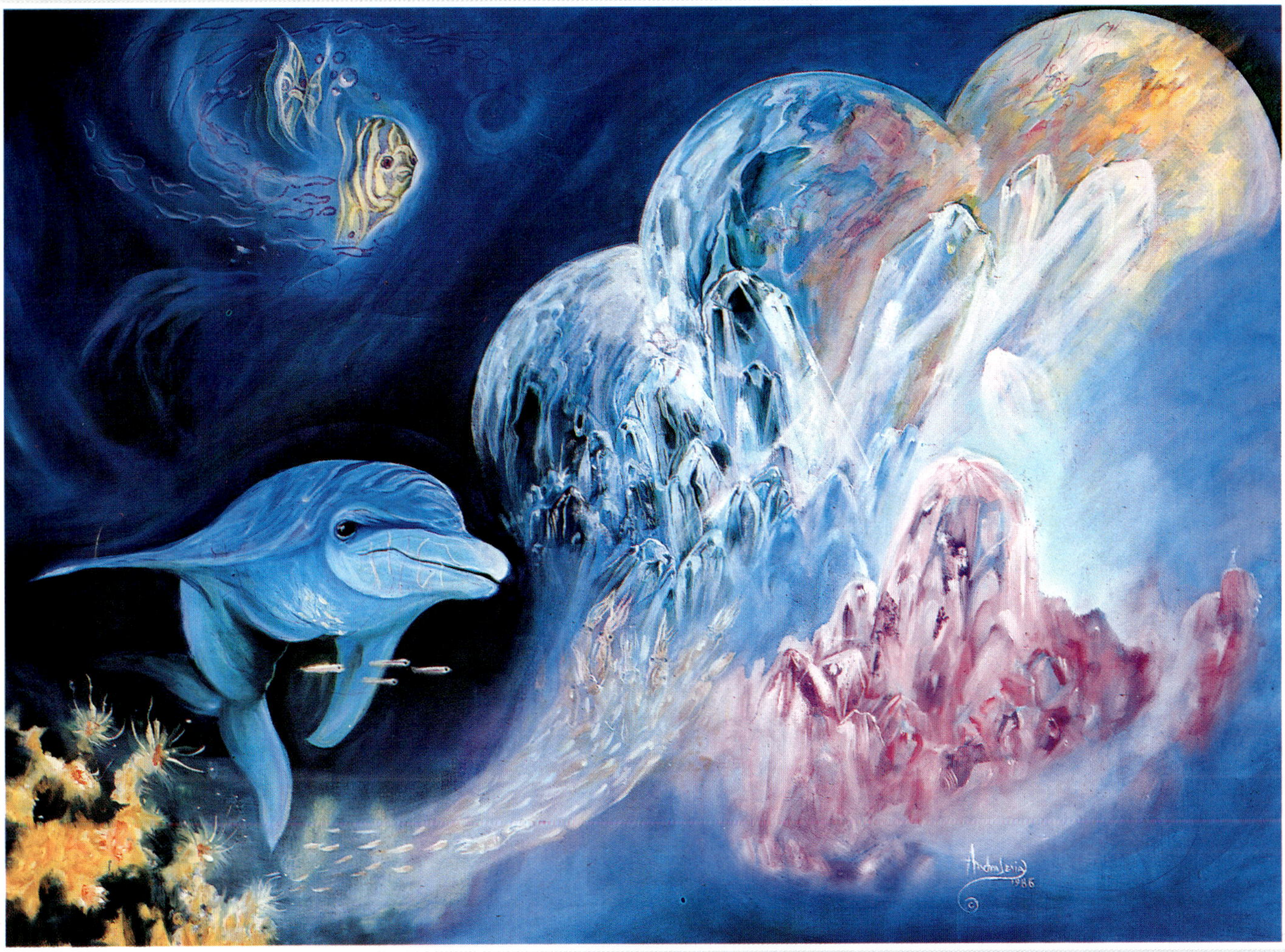

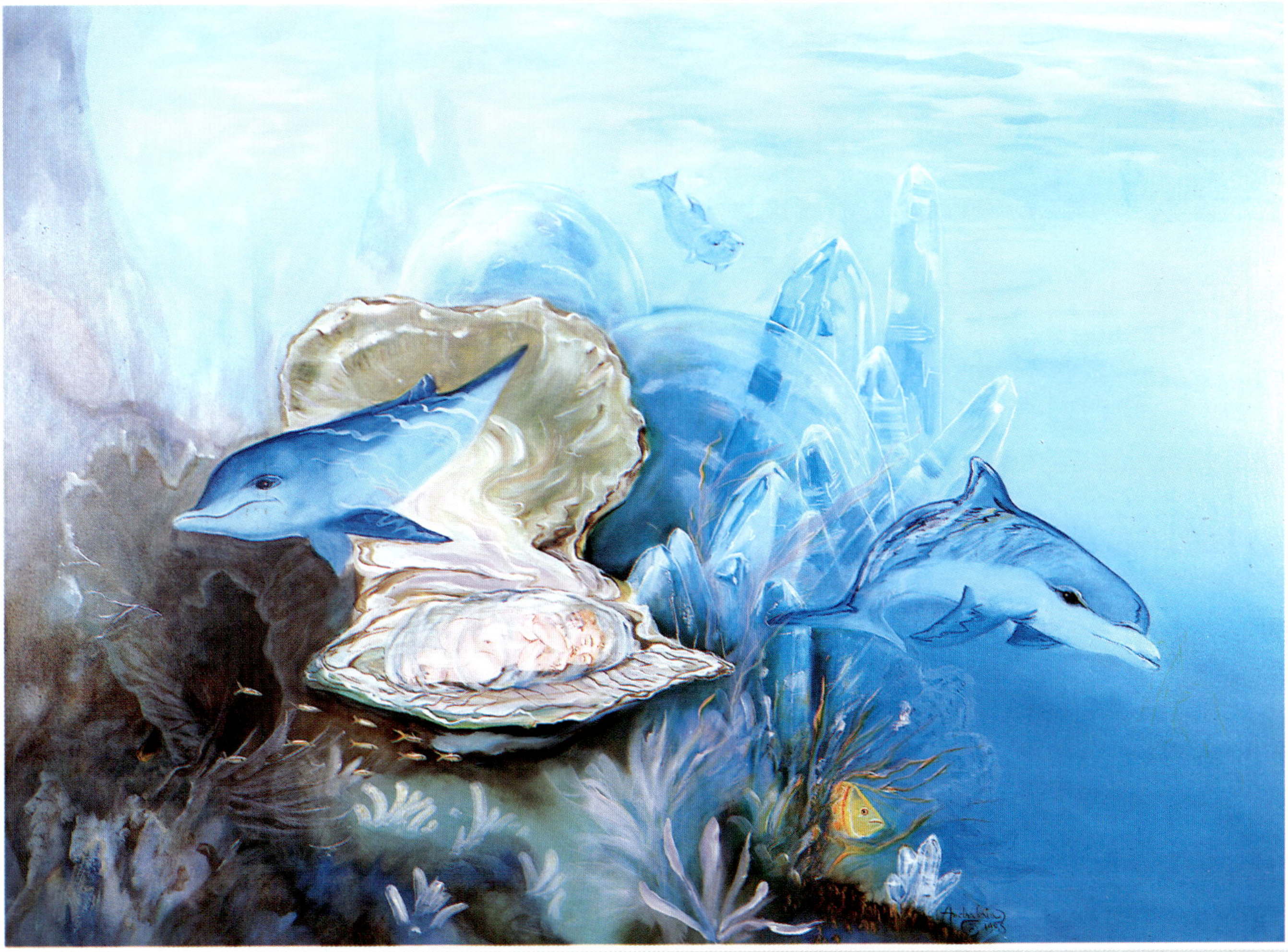

Cosmic Troubador
Andraleria

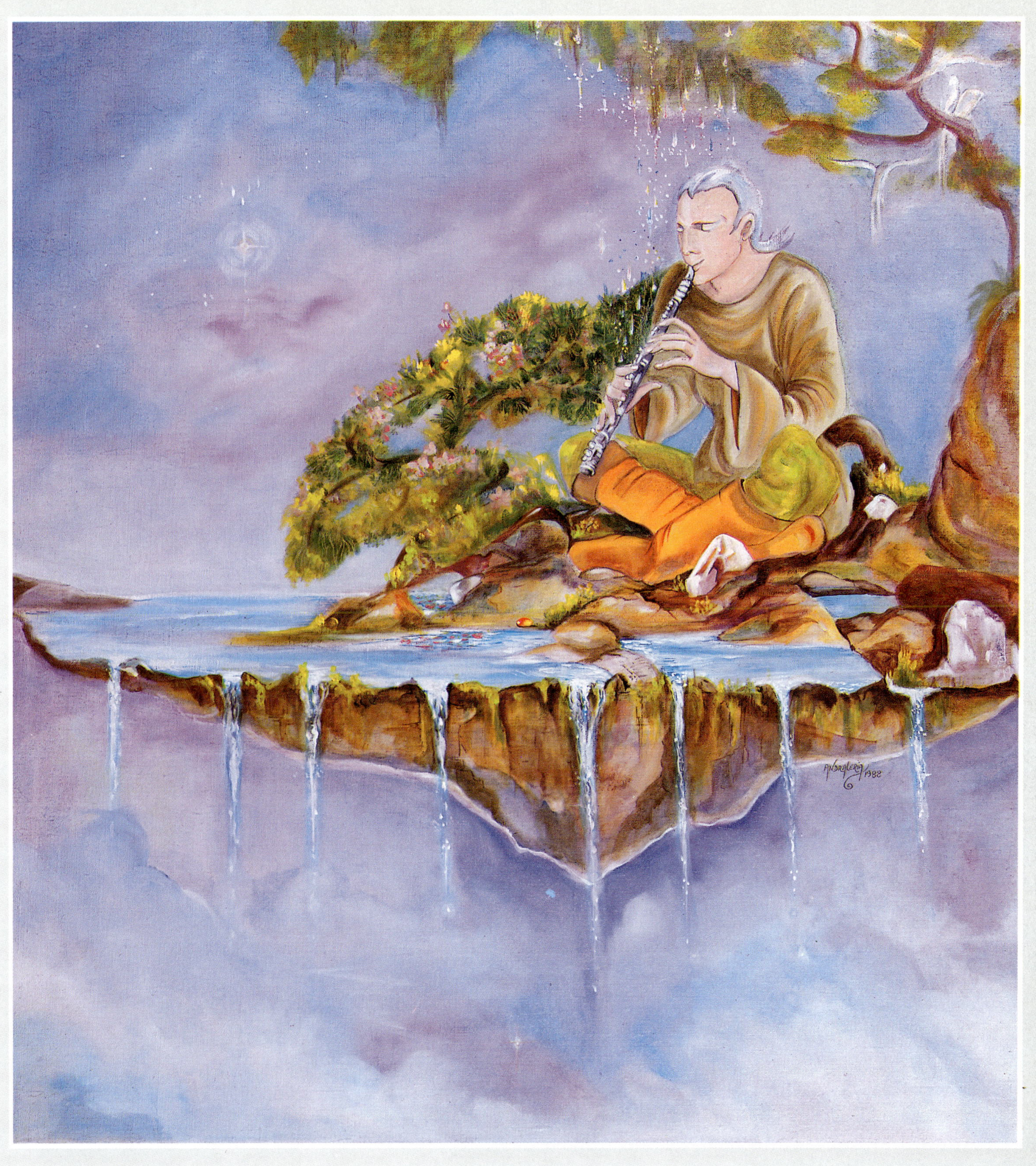

The Two Elves
Andraleria

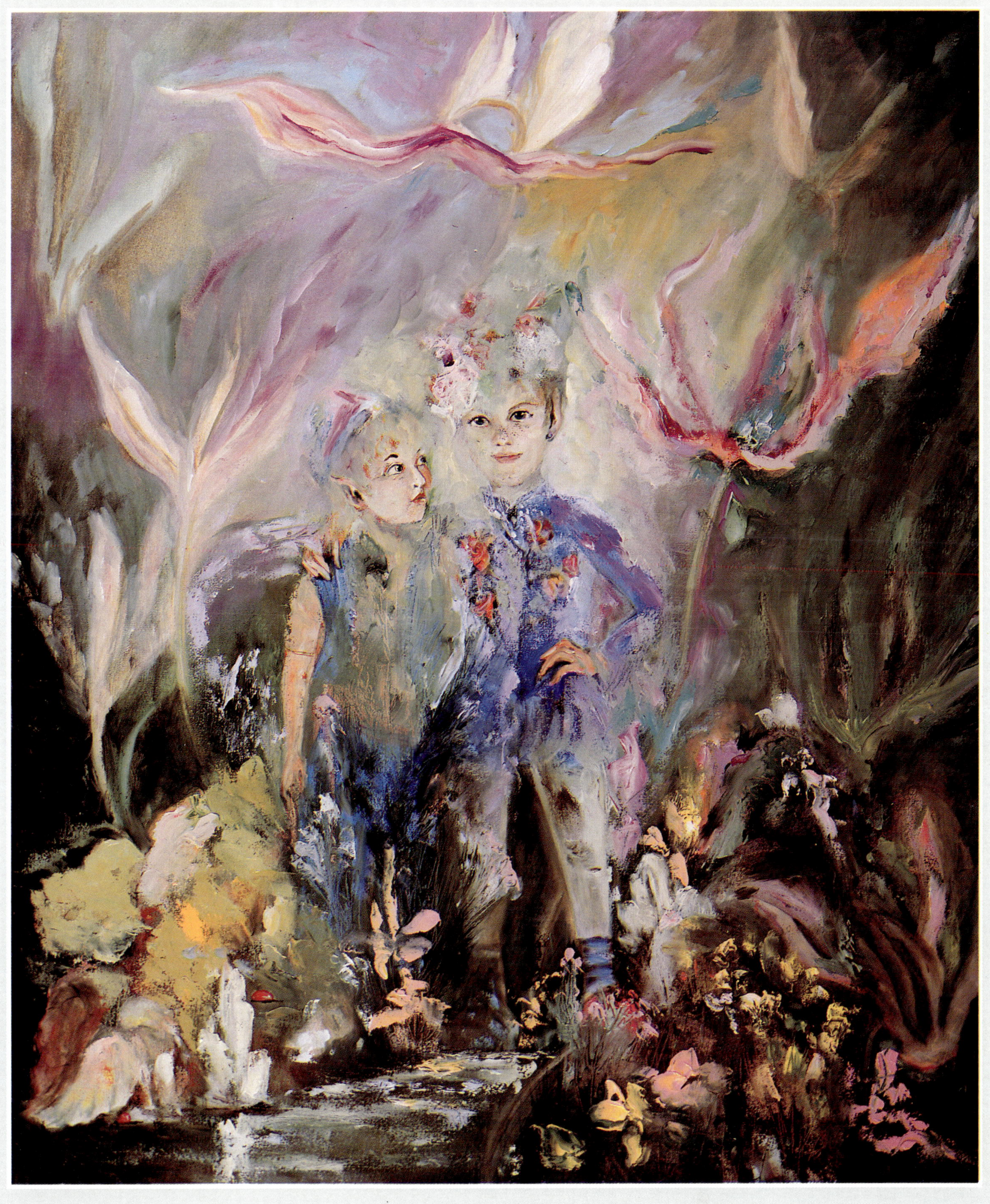

Spirit Flight
Andraleria

Spirit Woman
and the Rainbow Dolphins
Andraleria

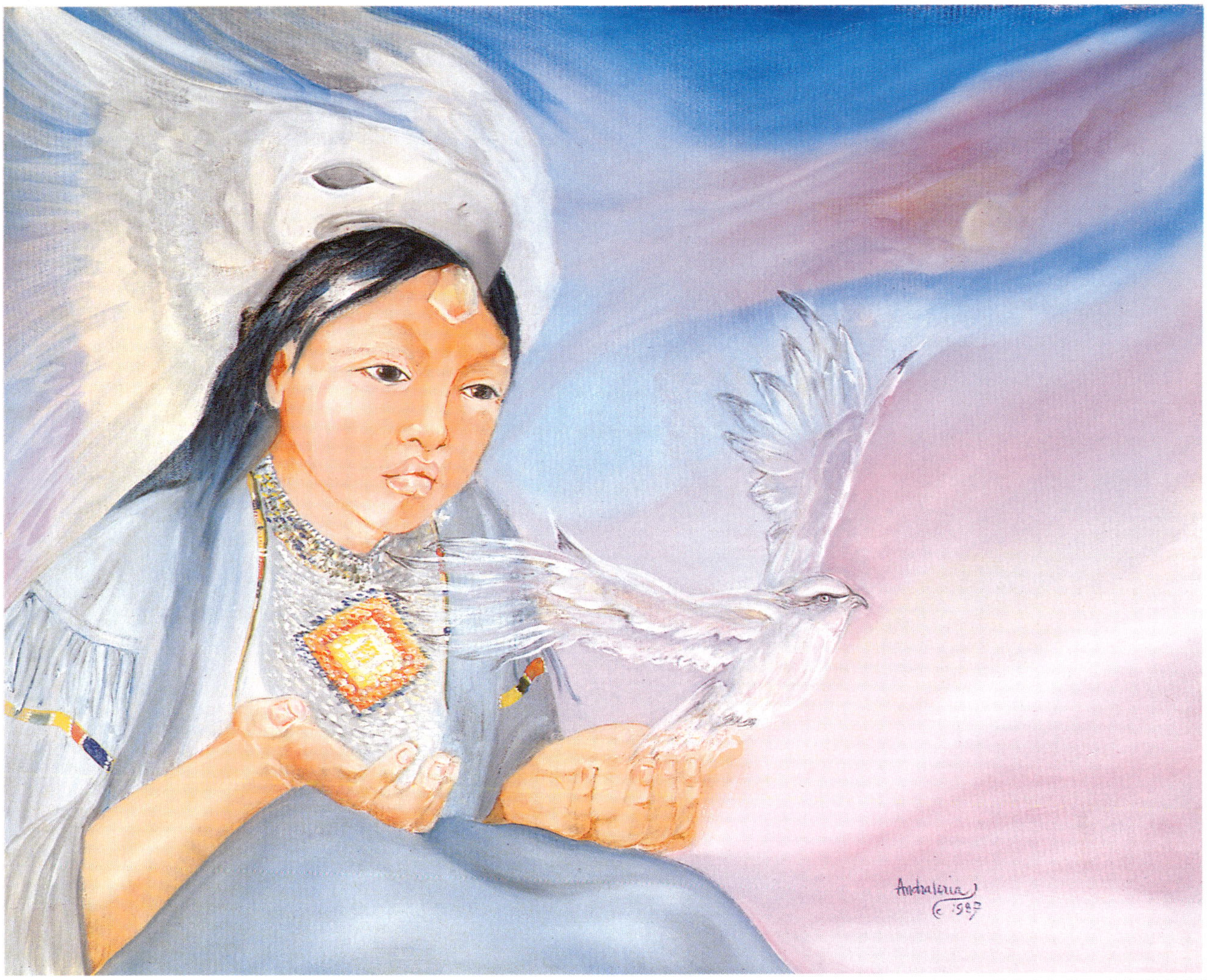

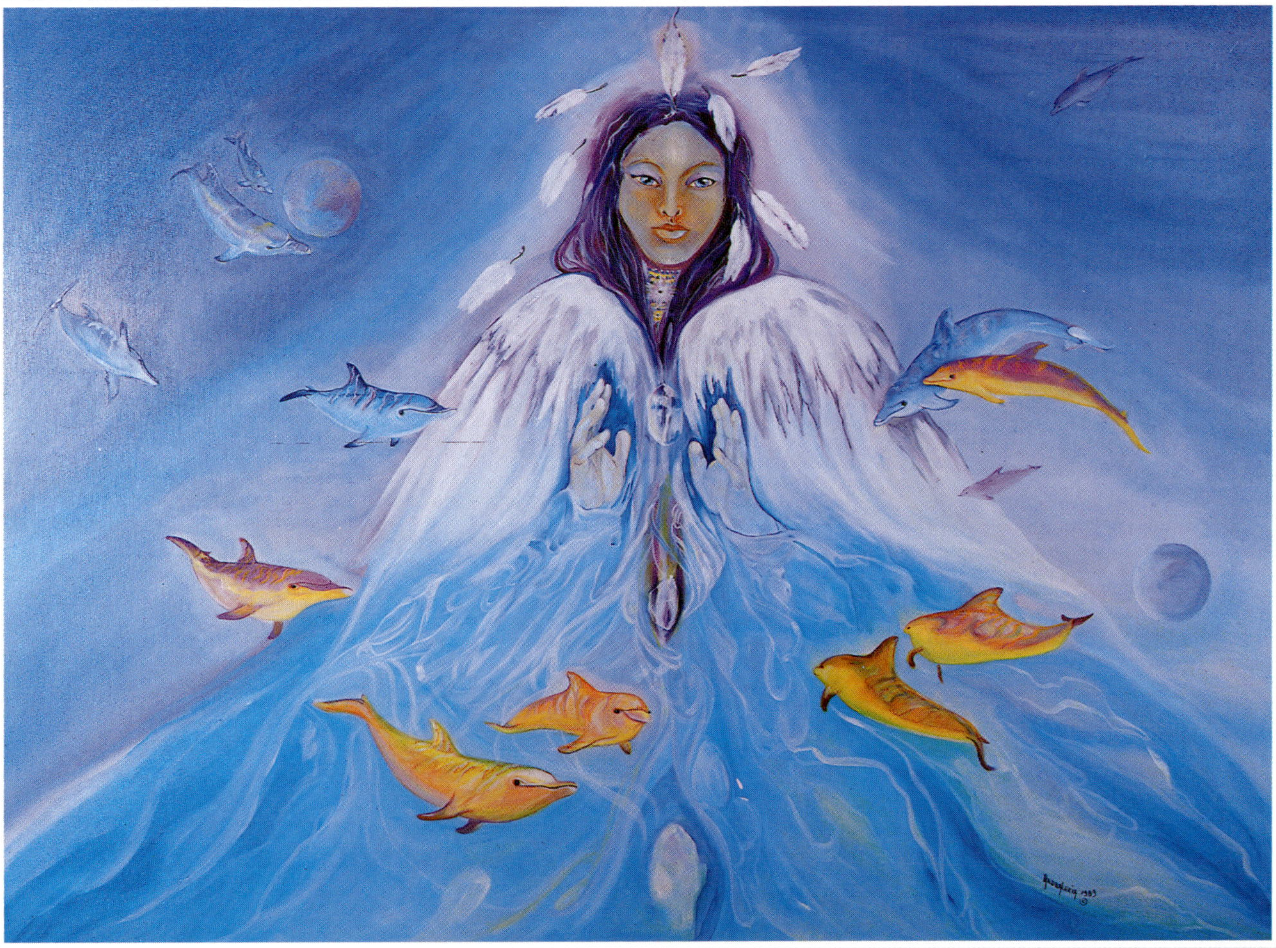

Diana and Apollo
Andraleria

Celestial Virgins
Andraleria

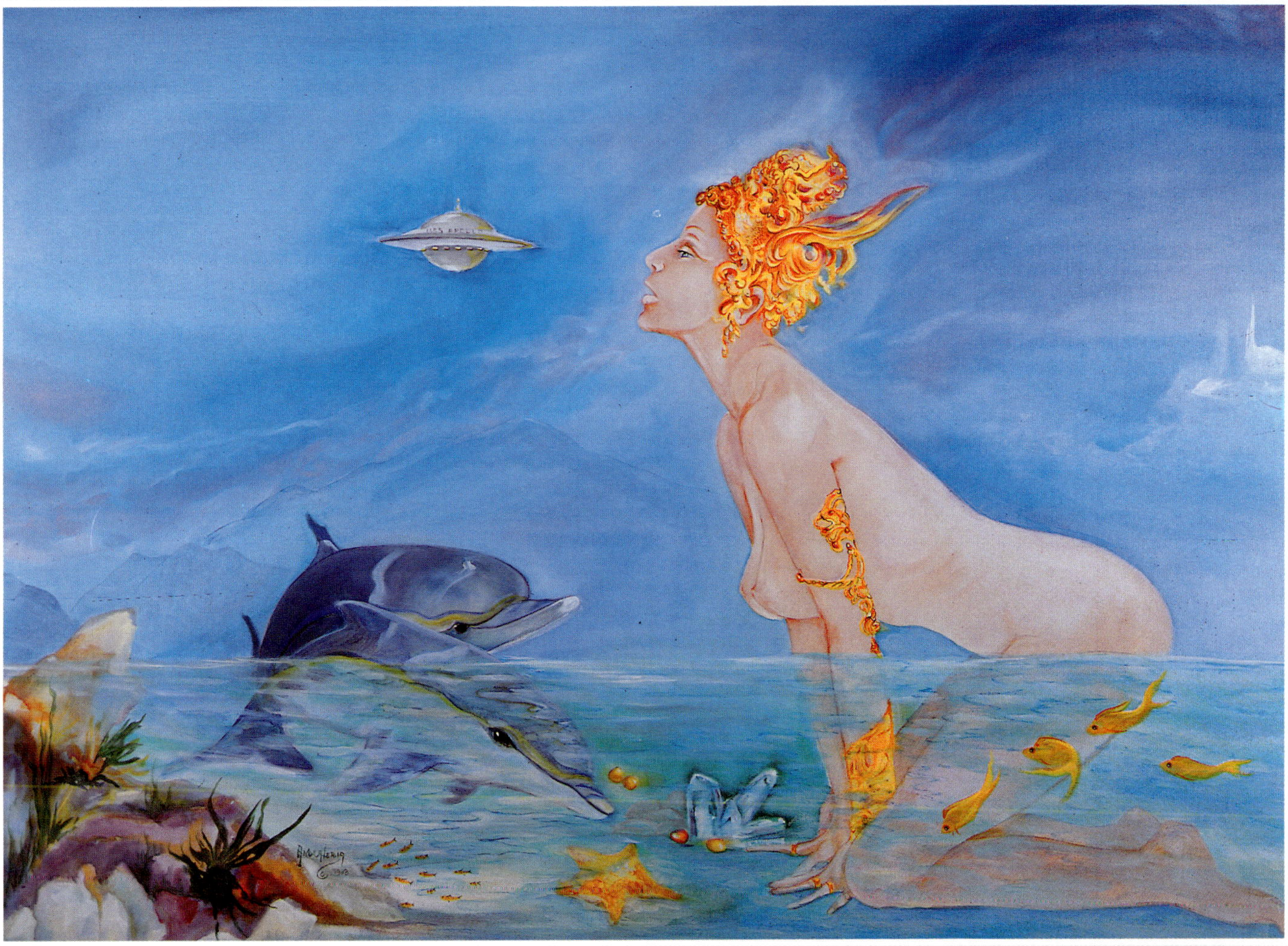

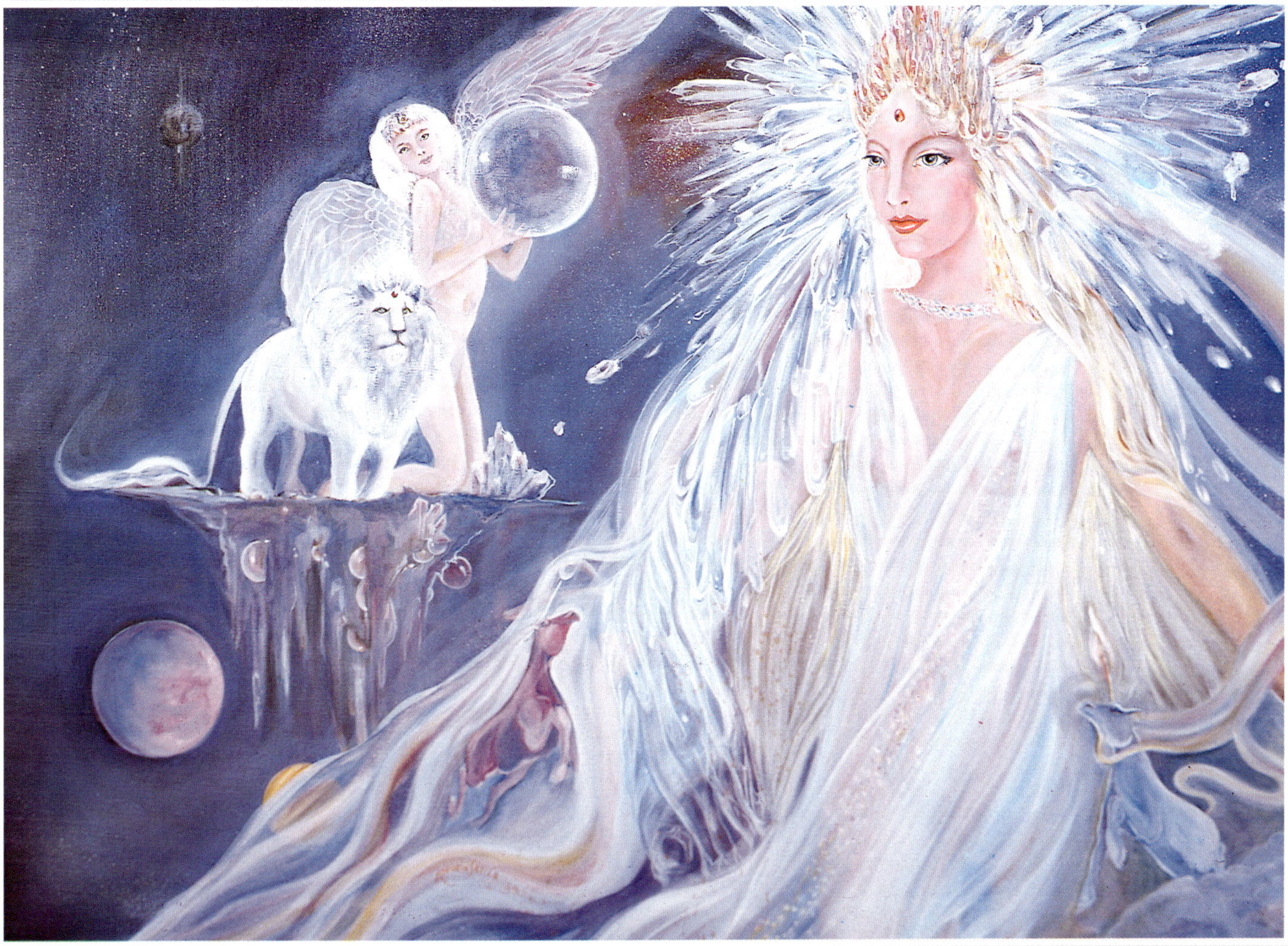

Wisdom Quest
Andraleria

Invoking the Goddess
Andraleria

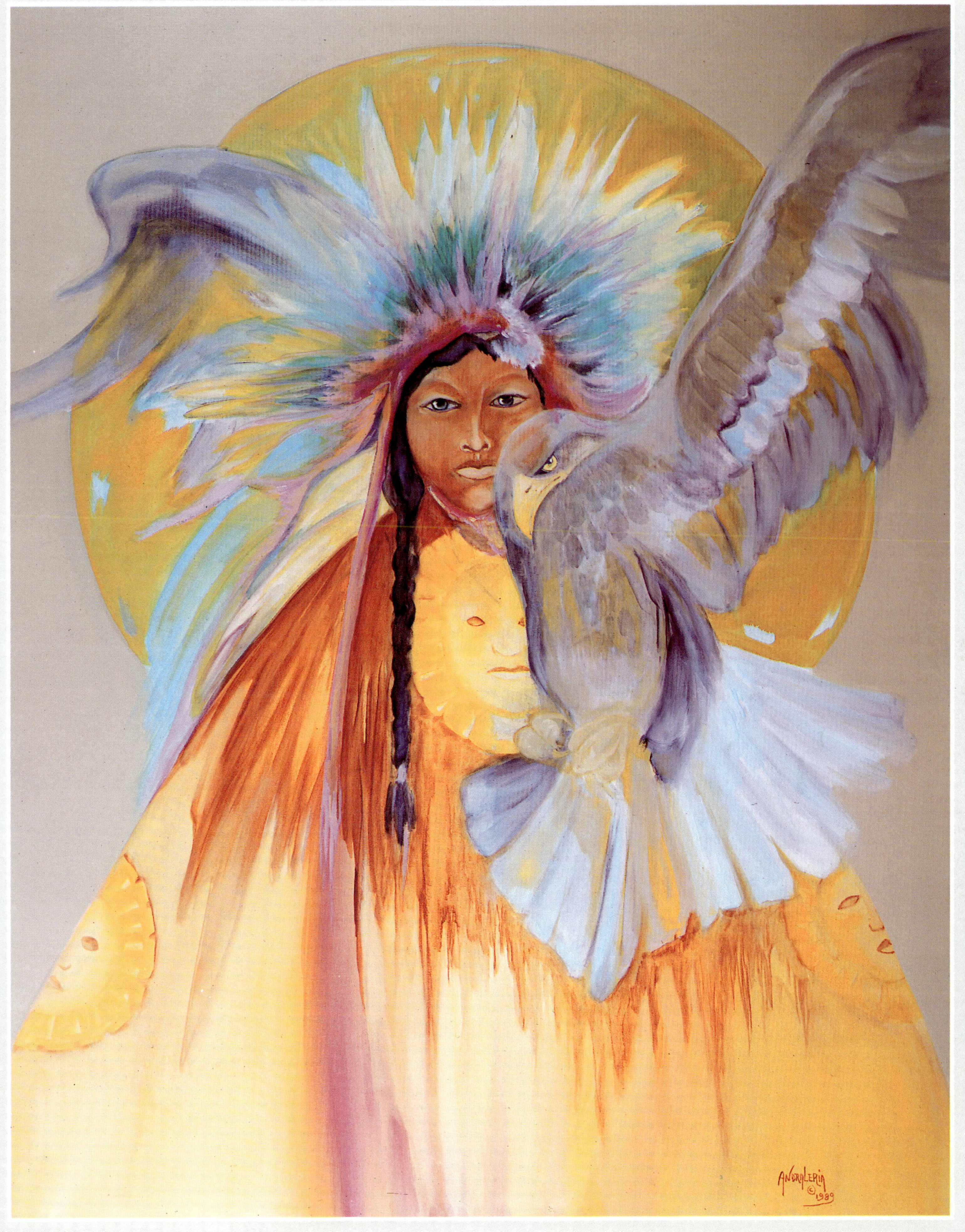
© 1989

Aquila
Andraleria

Medicine Man
Andraleria

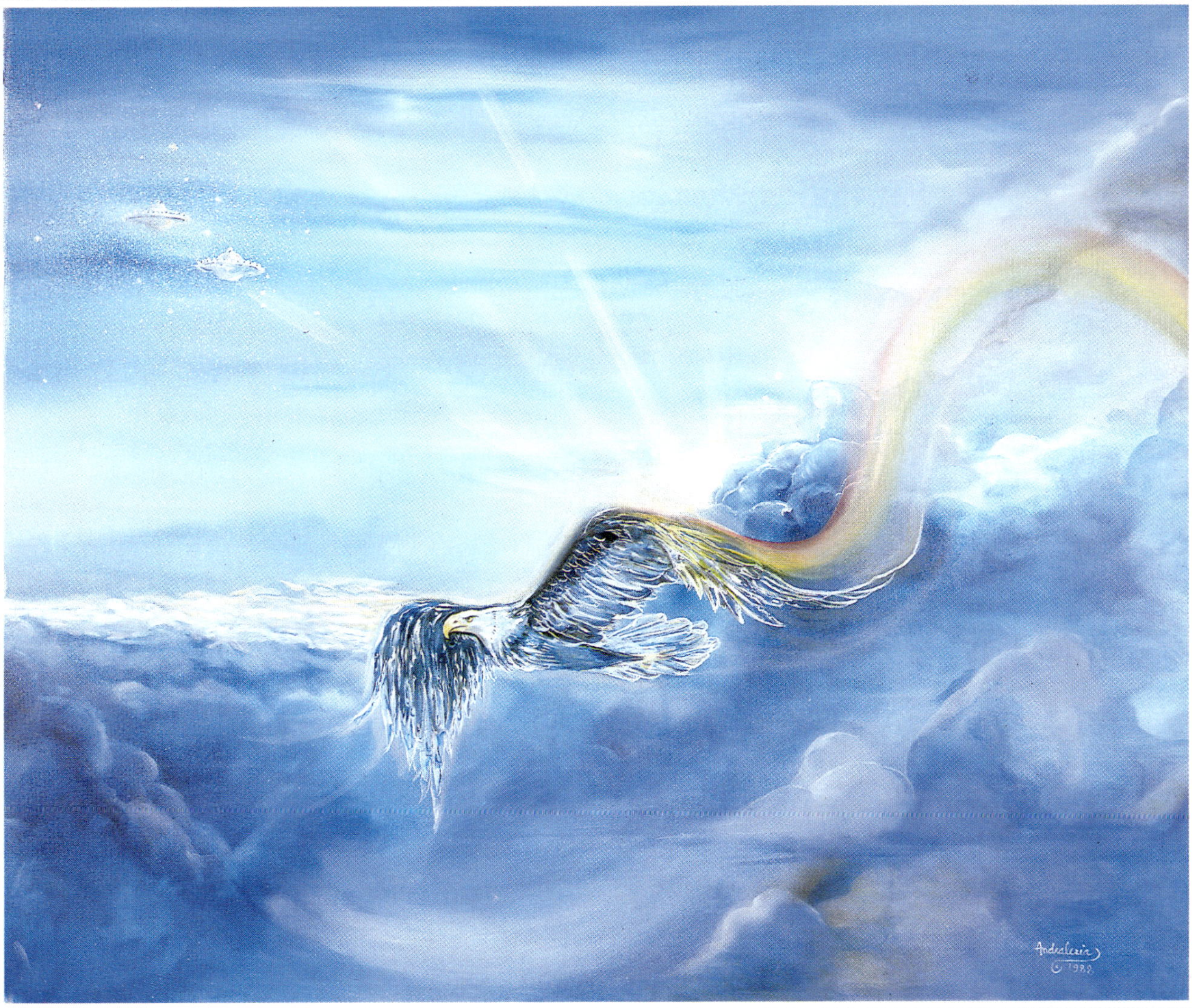

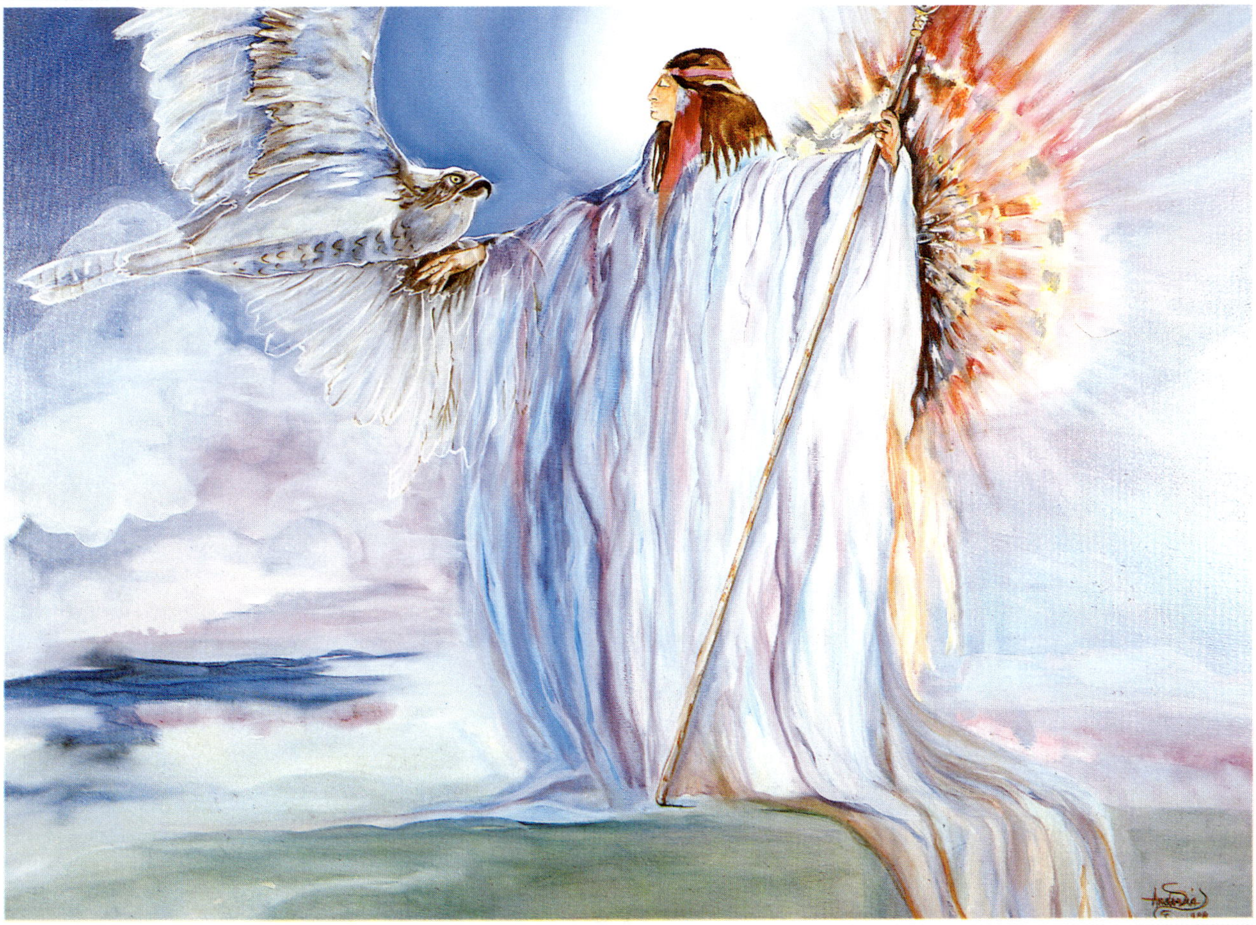

Devas of Mt. Shasta
Andraleria

Council of the B'enai Elohim
Andraleria

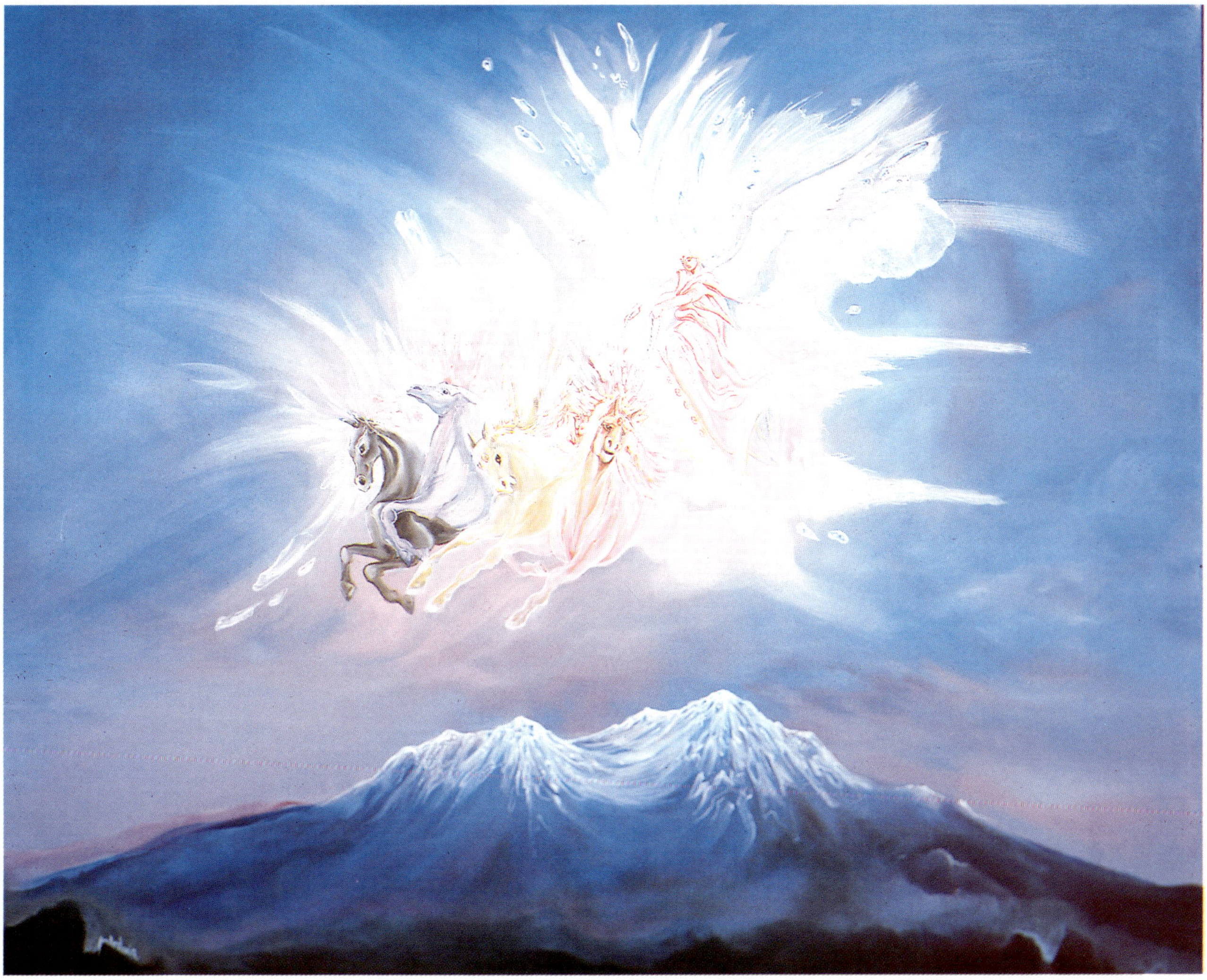

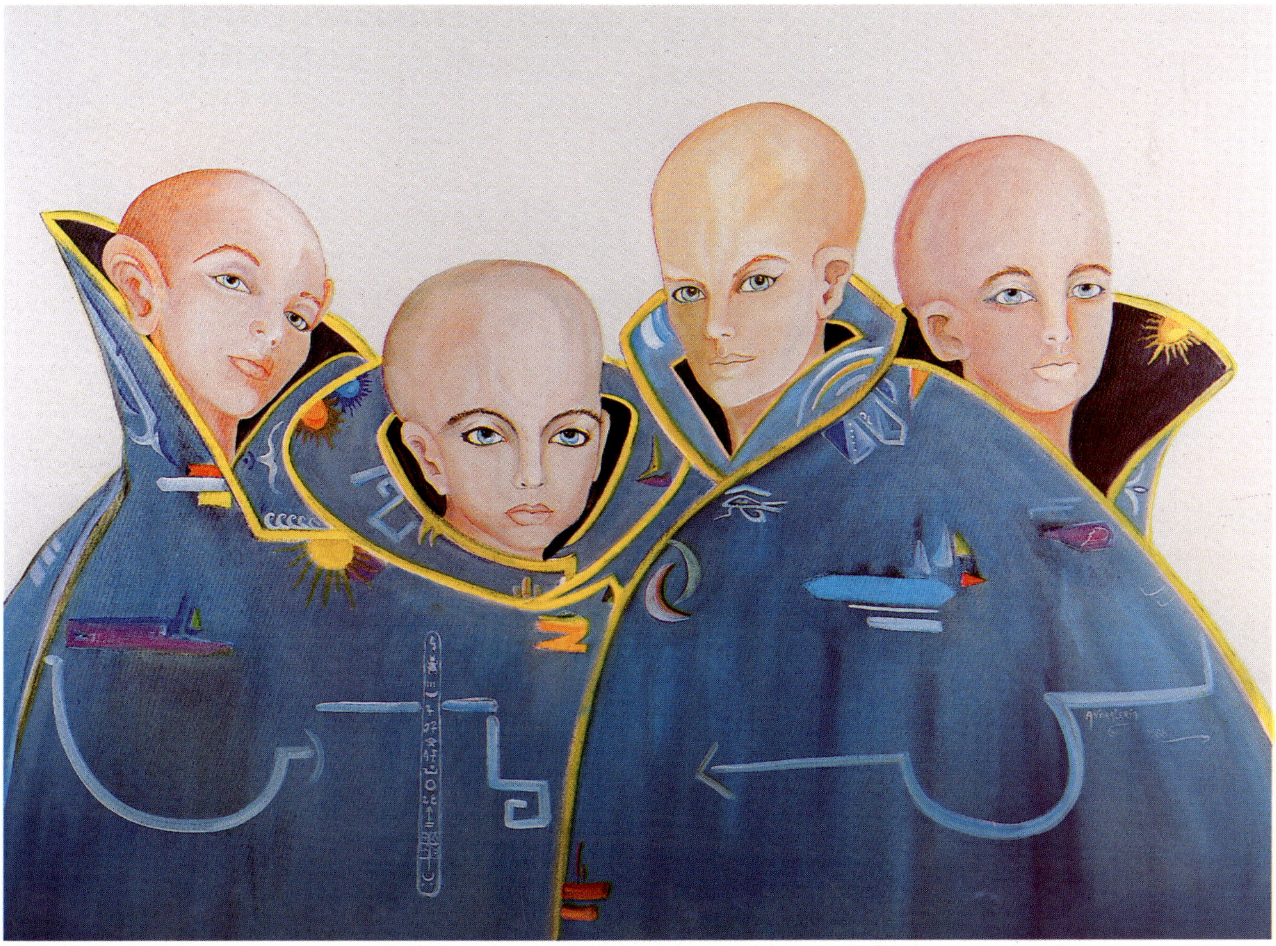

Astara-First Captain (L)
Andraleria

Aliah (R)
Andraleria

Emerzon-Captain (L)
Andraleria

Lai Tai Dru (R)
Andraleria

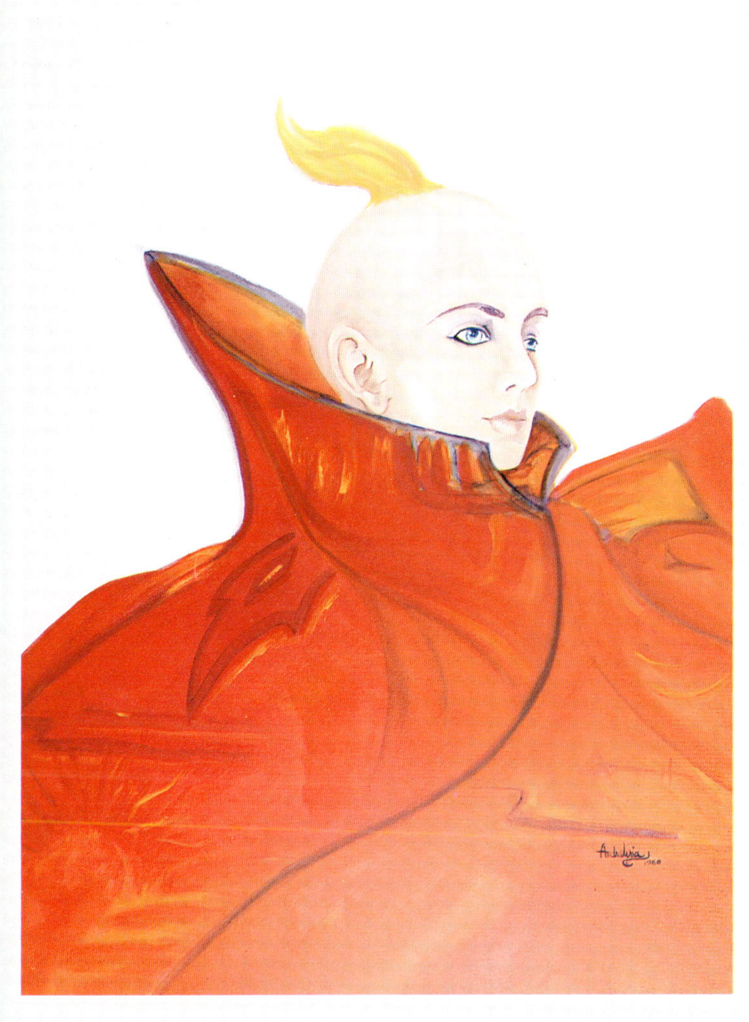

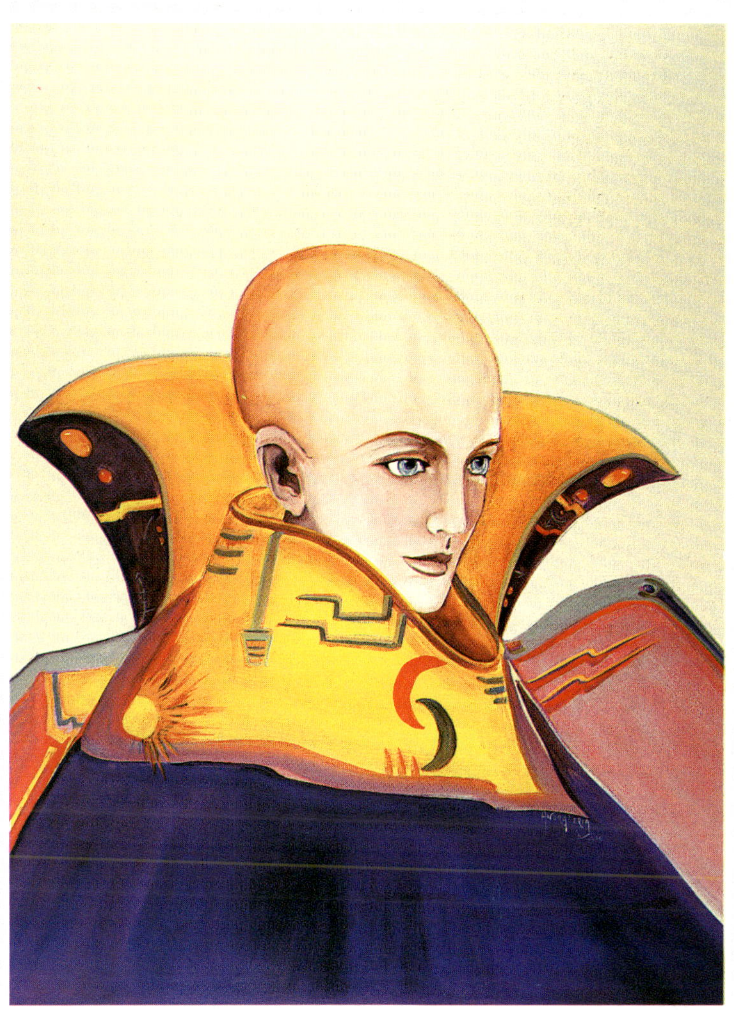

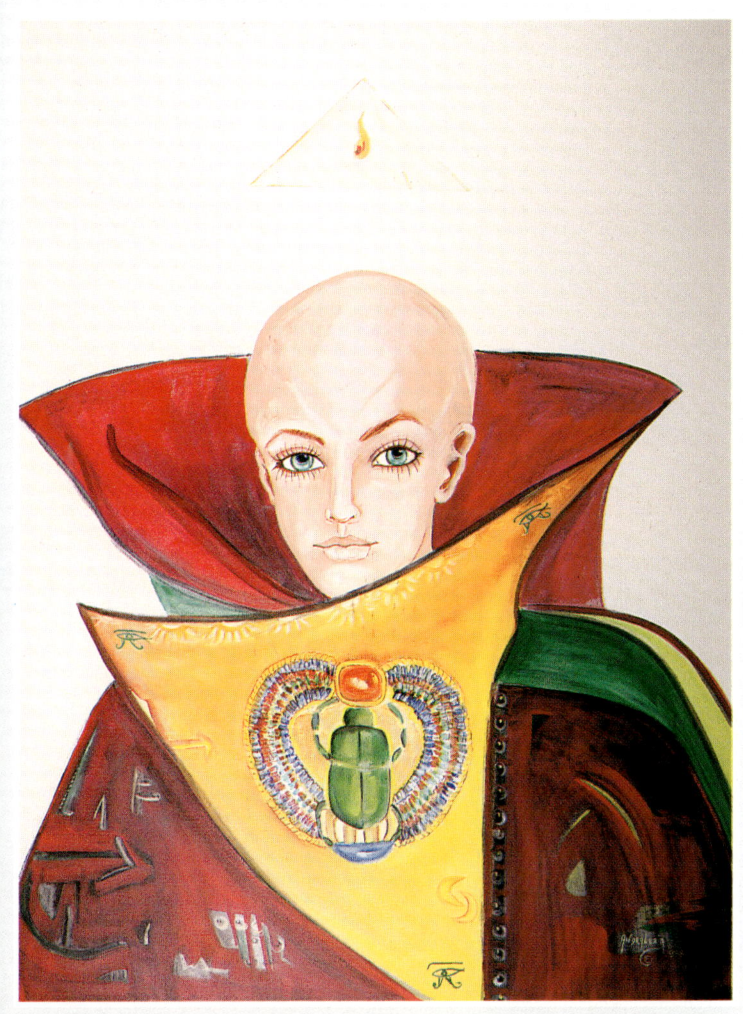

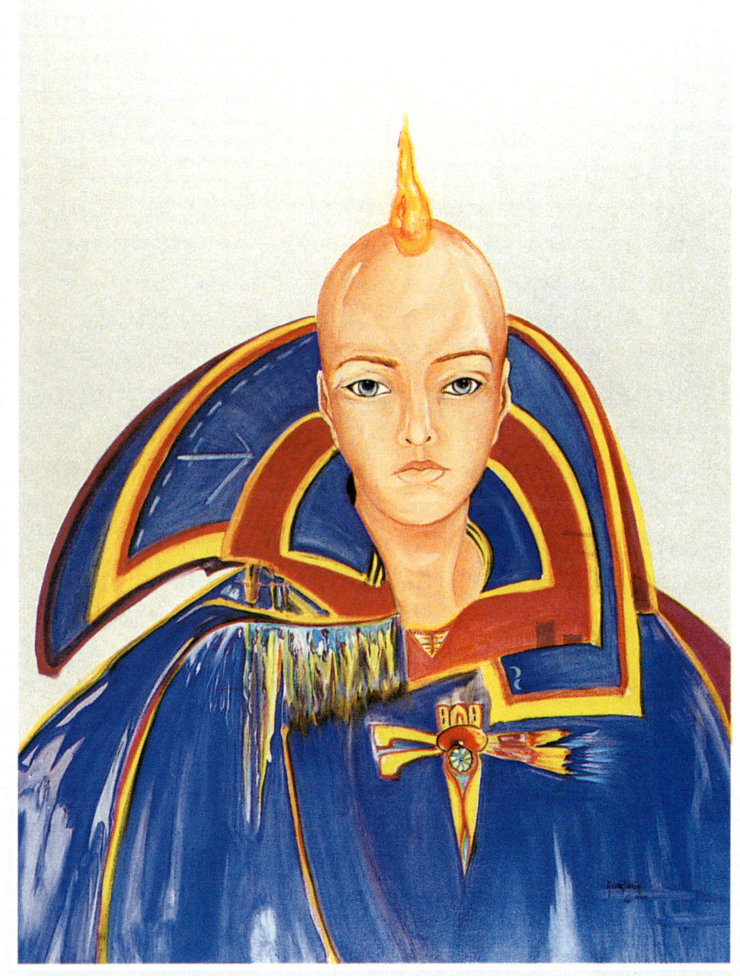

IXTHARA

Ixthara (Dutsei is her family nickname) was born in 1956 in Cleveland Ohio, the only daughter of very loving parents Marjorie and Edward Friedl. Because of the warm affection of her parents and grandparents (Dr. and Mrs. Friedl) she was able to attend many schools of learning and for many different subjects. She attended and graduated from Interlochen Arts Academy, Messiah College (she has a B.A. in religion studied 2 years of the original Greek and The Book of Revelation in the original), she attended the Welsh College of Music and Drama in Wales Great Britain (2 years), Cleveland Institute of Music, Cleveland Institute of Art and took advanced art at Cleveland State University.

Ixthara has studied Shakespeare, directing, voice, movement, dance, drums, music, writing, poetry (she was with the poetry league of greater Cleveland for 2 years) and acting (she's been in at least 20 plays). She is also a "proud mom" and enjoys her daughter Anna. Besides all this she finds herself in retreats (a 50-day retreat recently) with Vajrayana Tibetan Buddhists learning ancient secrets she won't even speak about. Actually she is quite articulate and enjoys a good verbal exchange. Her art work takes on the scope of her learning. She lets her human limitations and her concepts go, and sees worlds most of us cannot imagine. She would most likely say anyone could if they tried to. Ixthara says: "My visions are actually not "mine." I have found that there is a great sharing going on, and that there truly is no seperation between the minds of others and my own mind. Many people tell me that the places I paint are the places they dream of."

In the future, Ixthara plans to just keep painting. She says "I like to do work that doesn't harm anyone. I would hope that our world would learn kindness; if you treat the world and everything in it with kindness no harm will come of it.

Celestial Mountain Lake
Ixthara

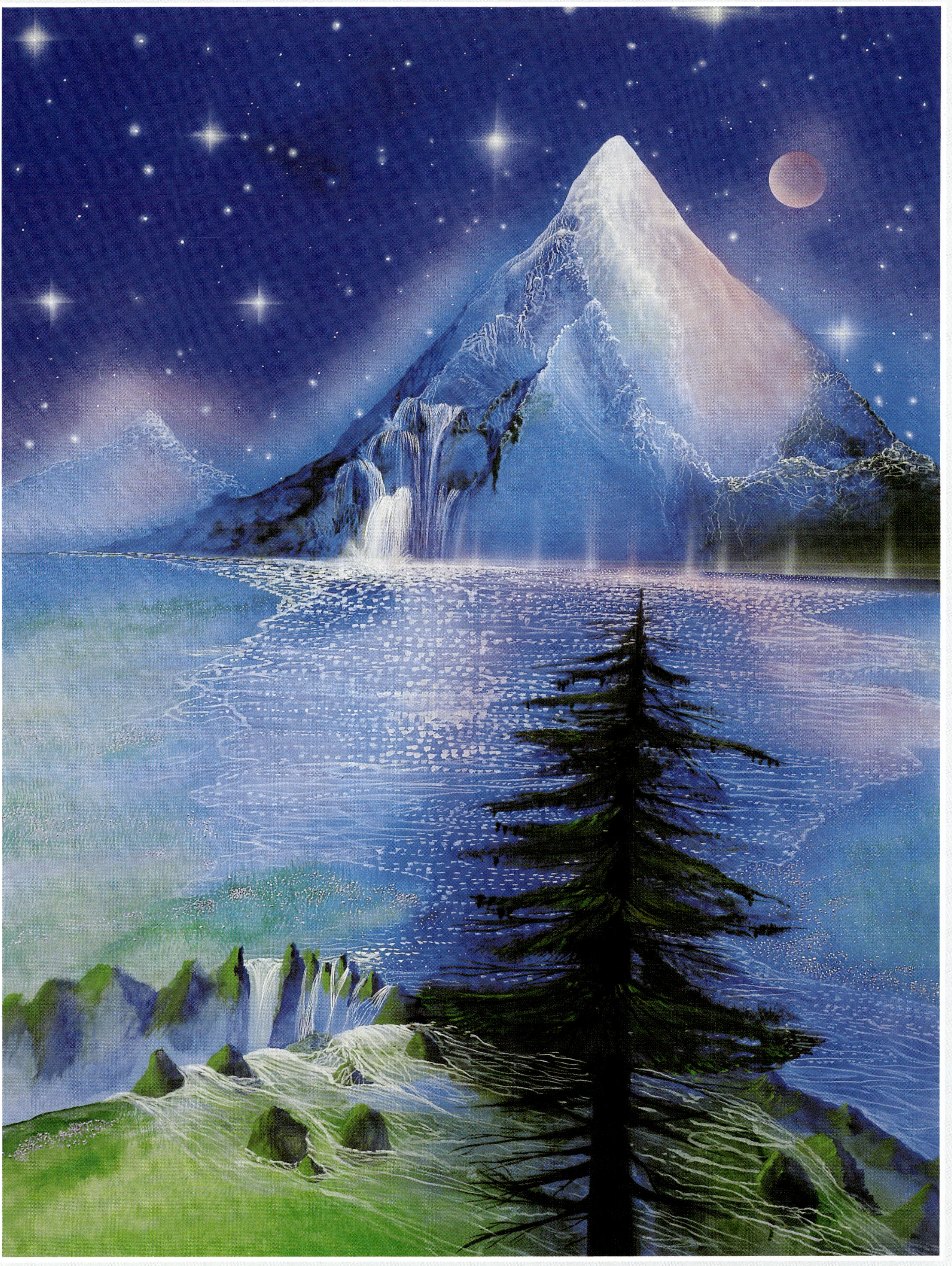

Wish Fulfilling Trees
Ixthara

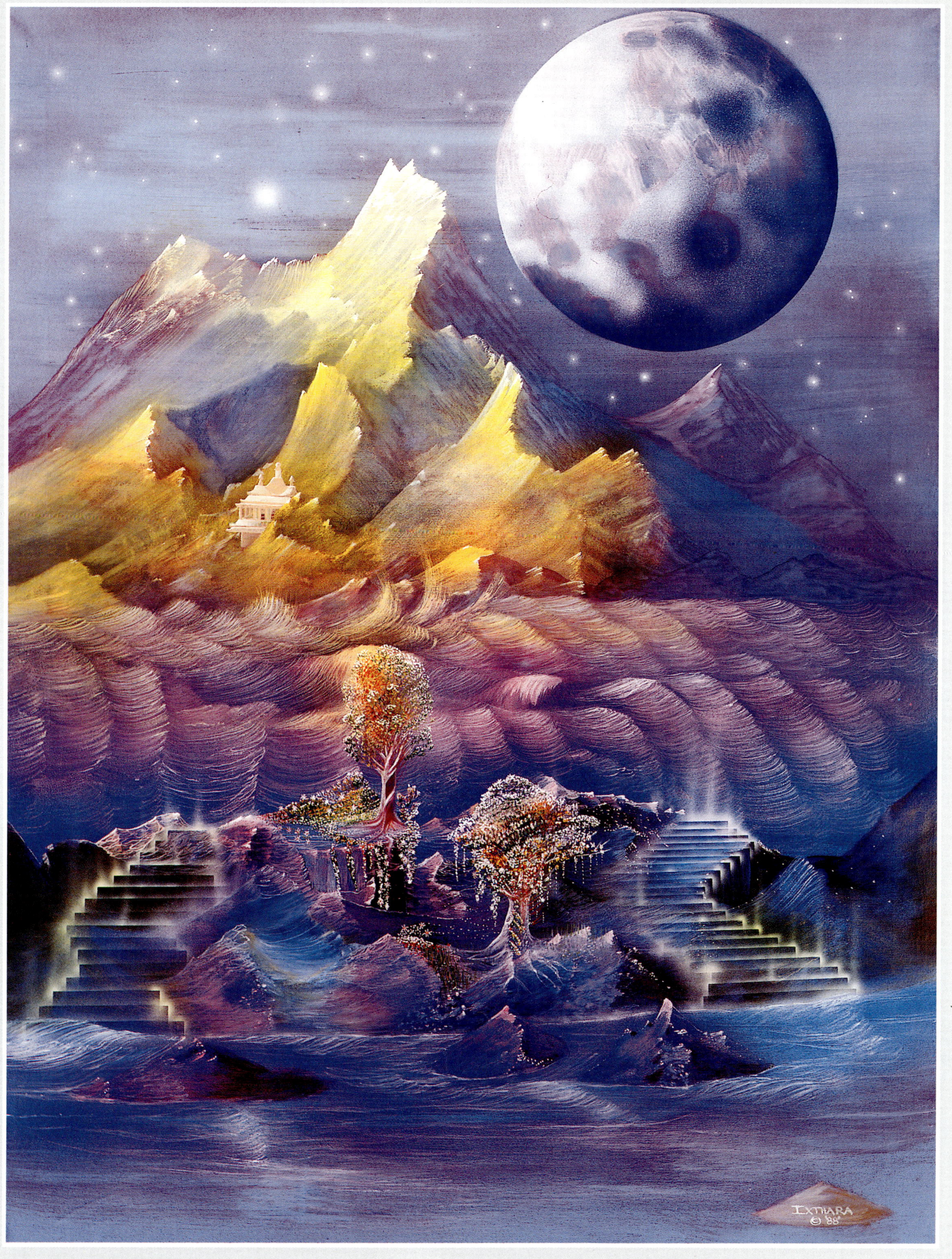
IXTIARA
© '88

Tiers of Healing Water
Ixthara

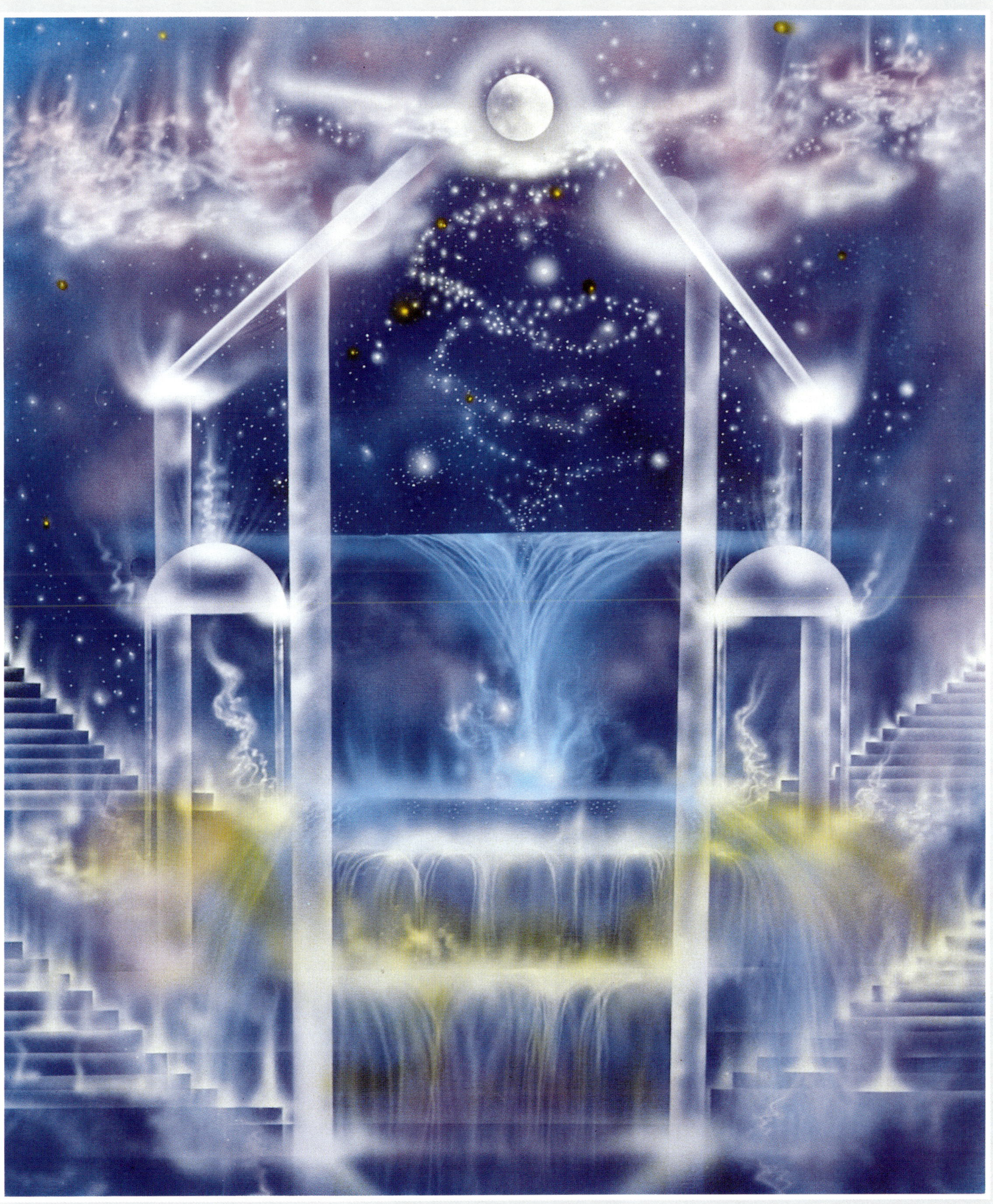

On Lotus Pond
Ixthara

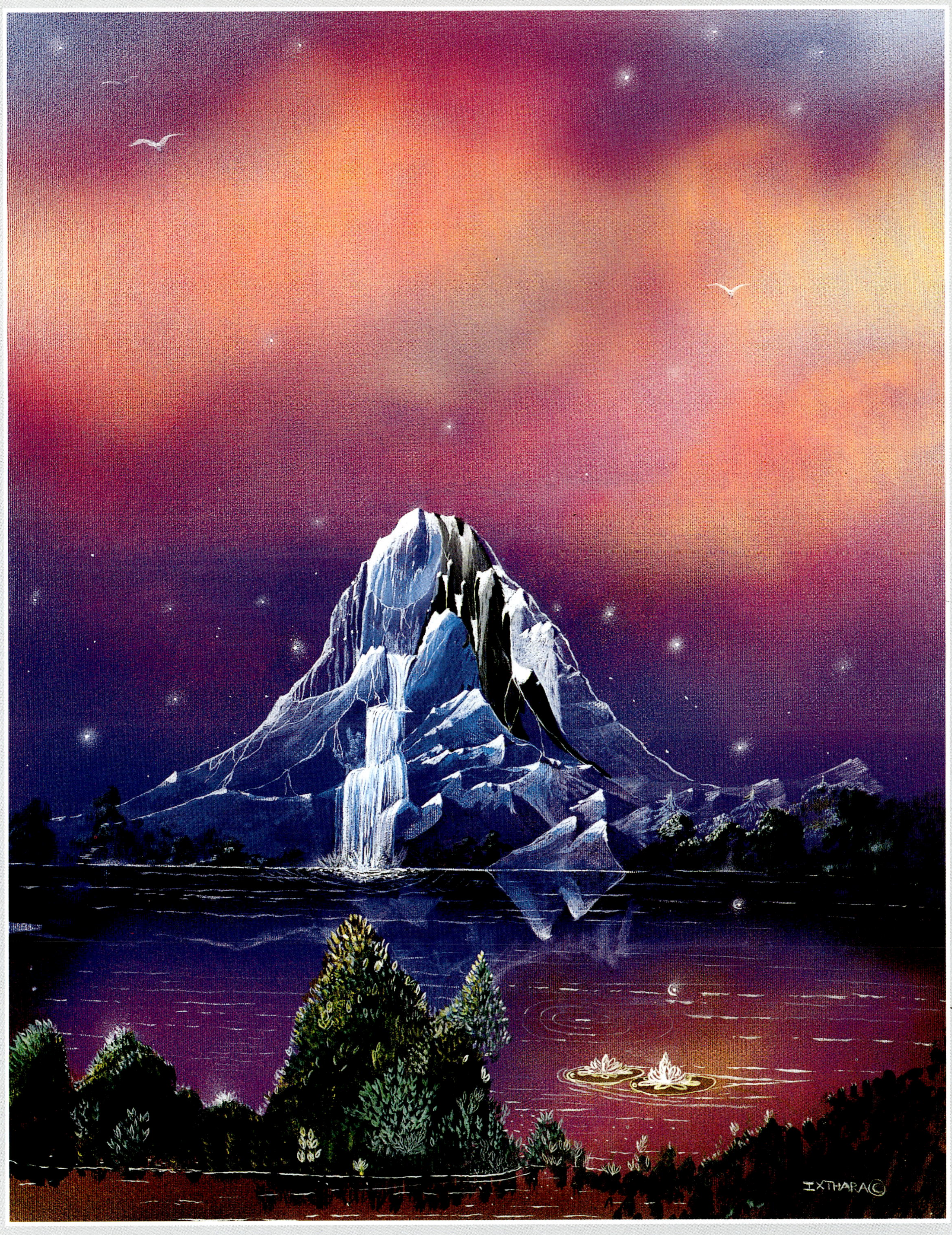
IXTHARA©

Star Medicine Woman
Ixthara

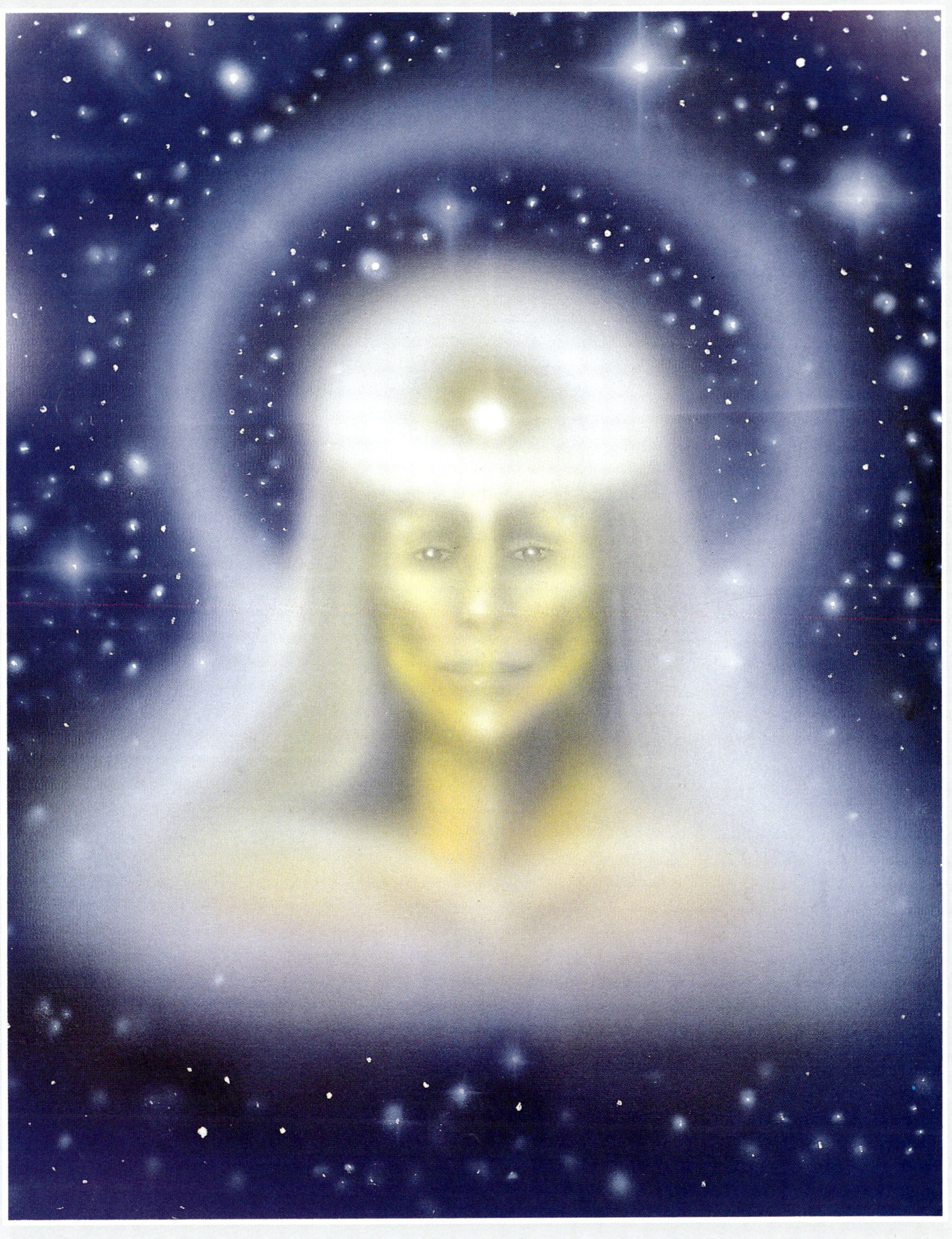

Petal Pond Devas
Ixthara

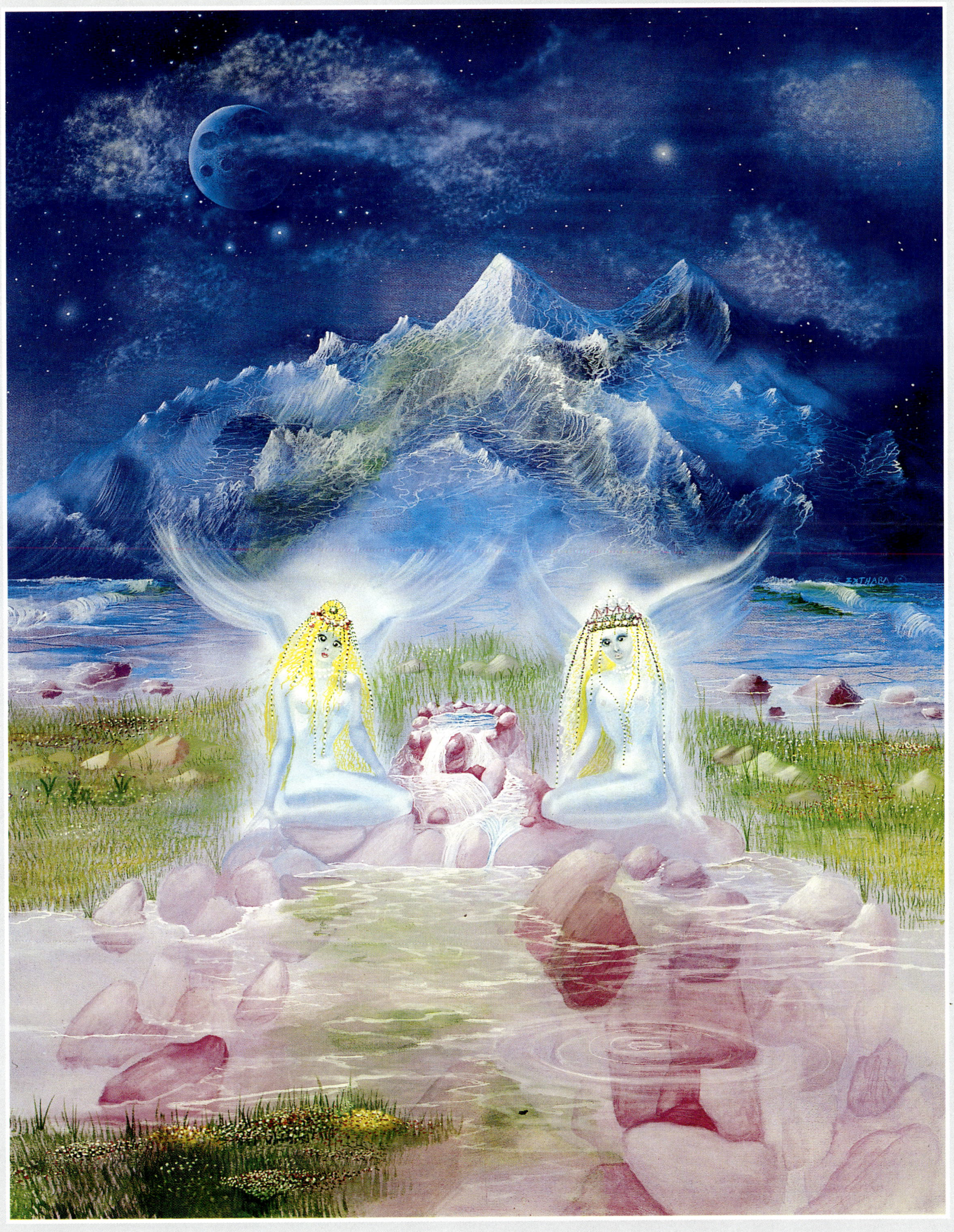

Infinity Flame
Ixthara

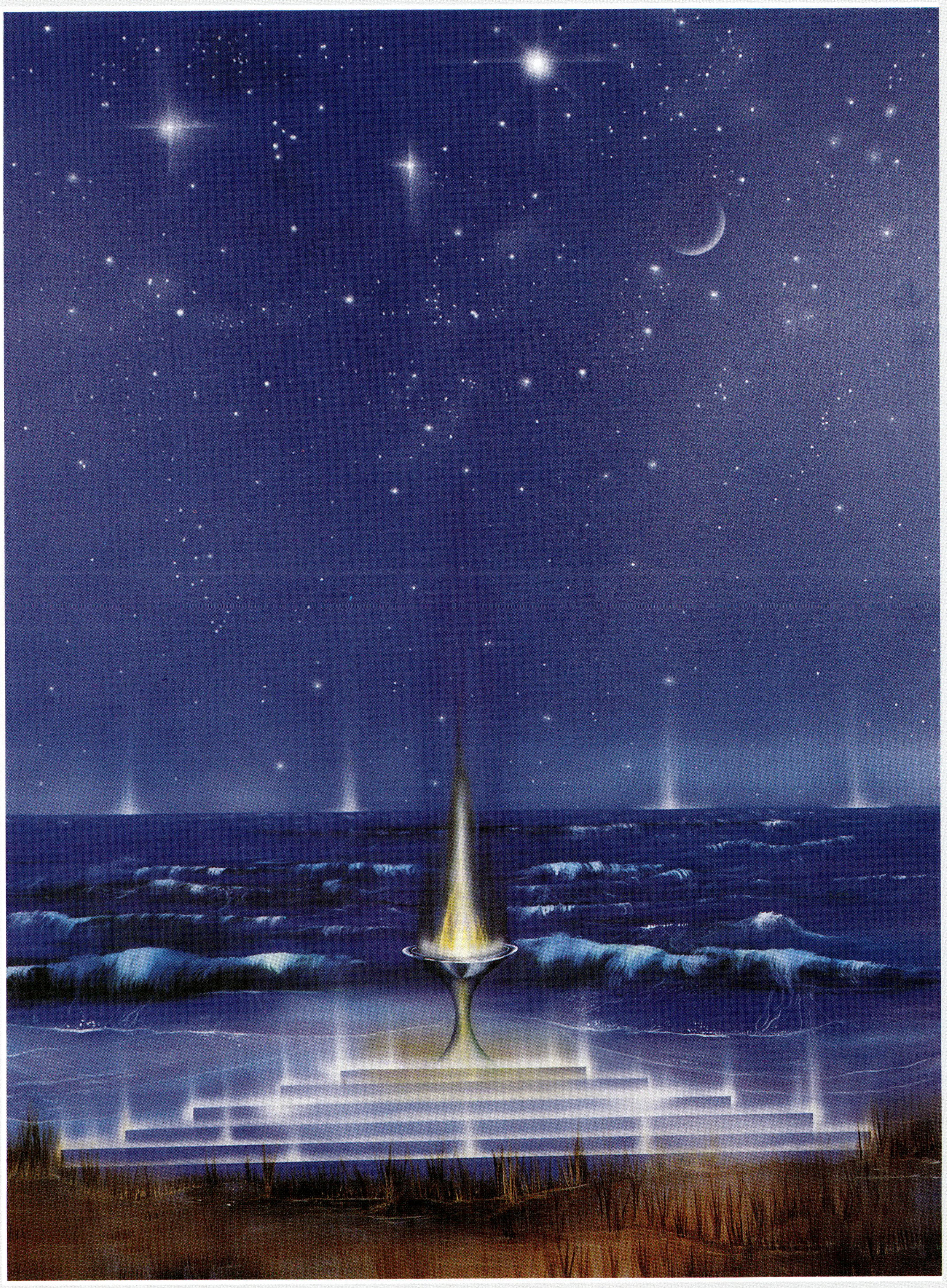

Emerald Tourmaline Falls
Ixthara

Twin Sceptered Mountain
Ixthara

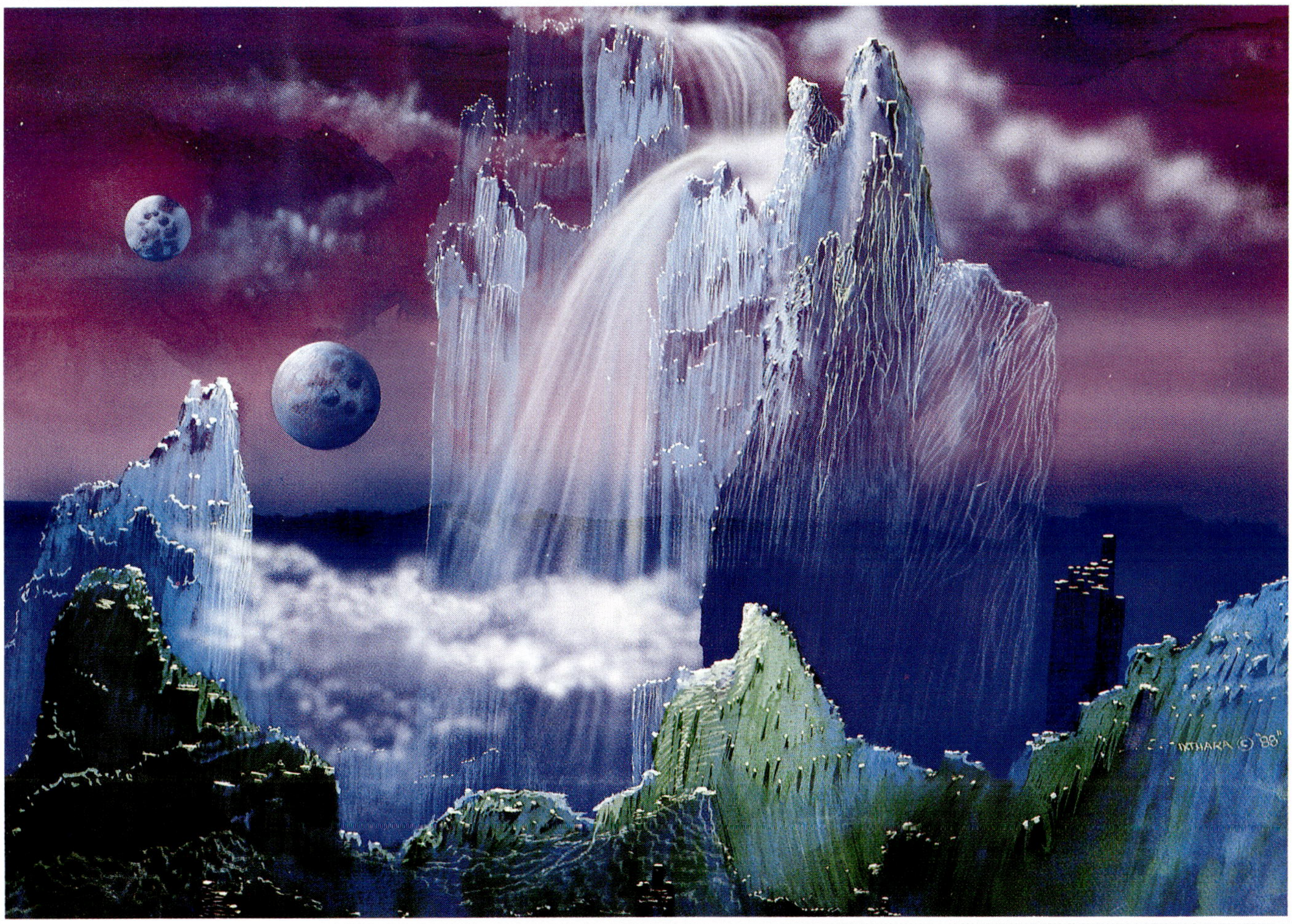

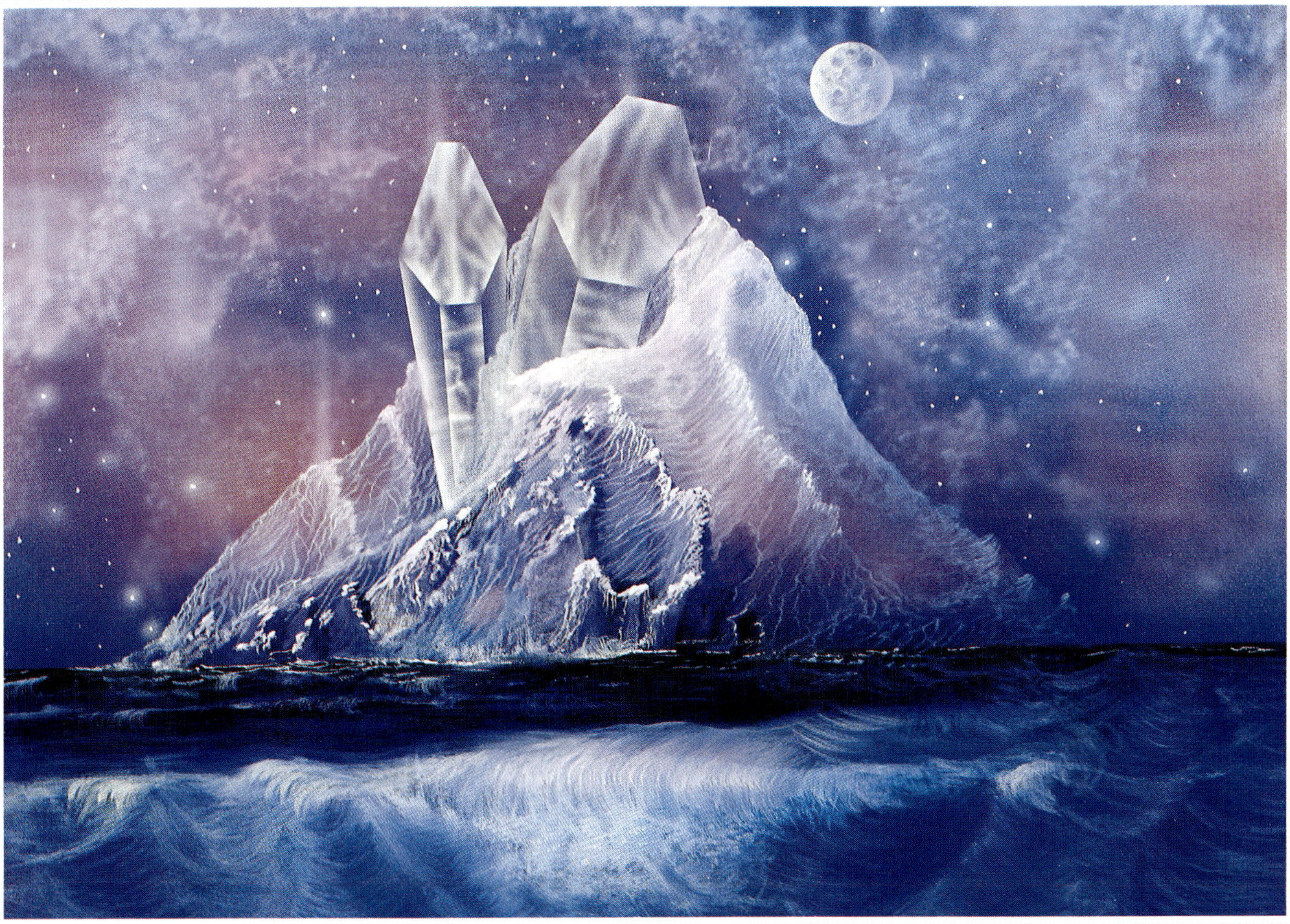

Temple of the Solar Angel
Ixthara

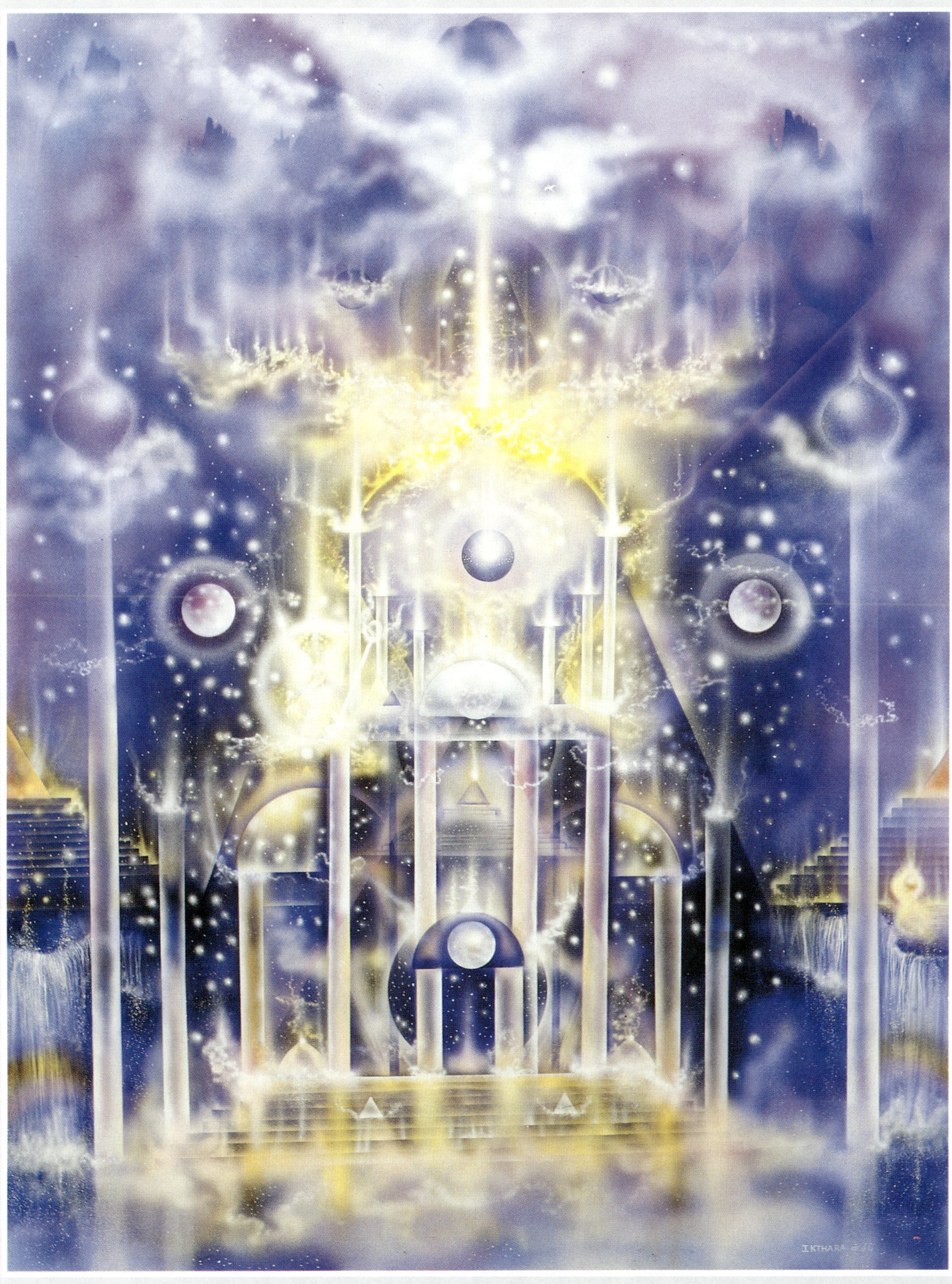

Orca Bay
Ixthara

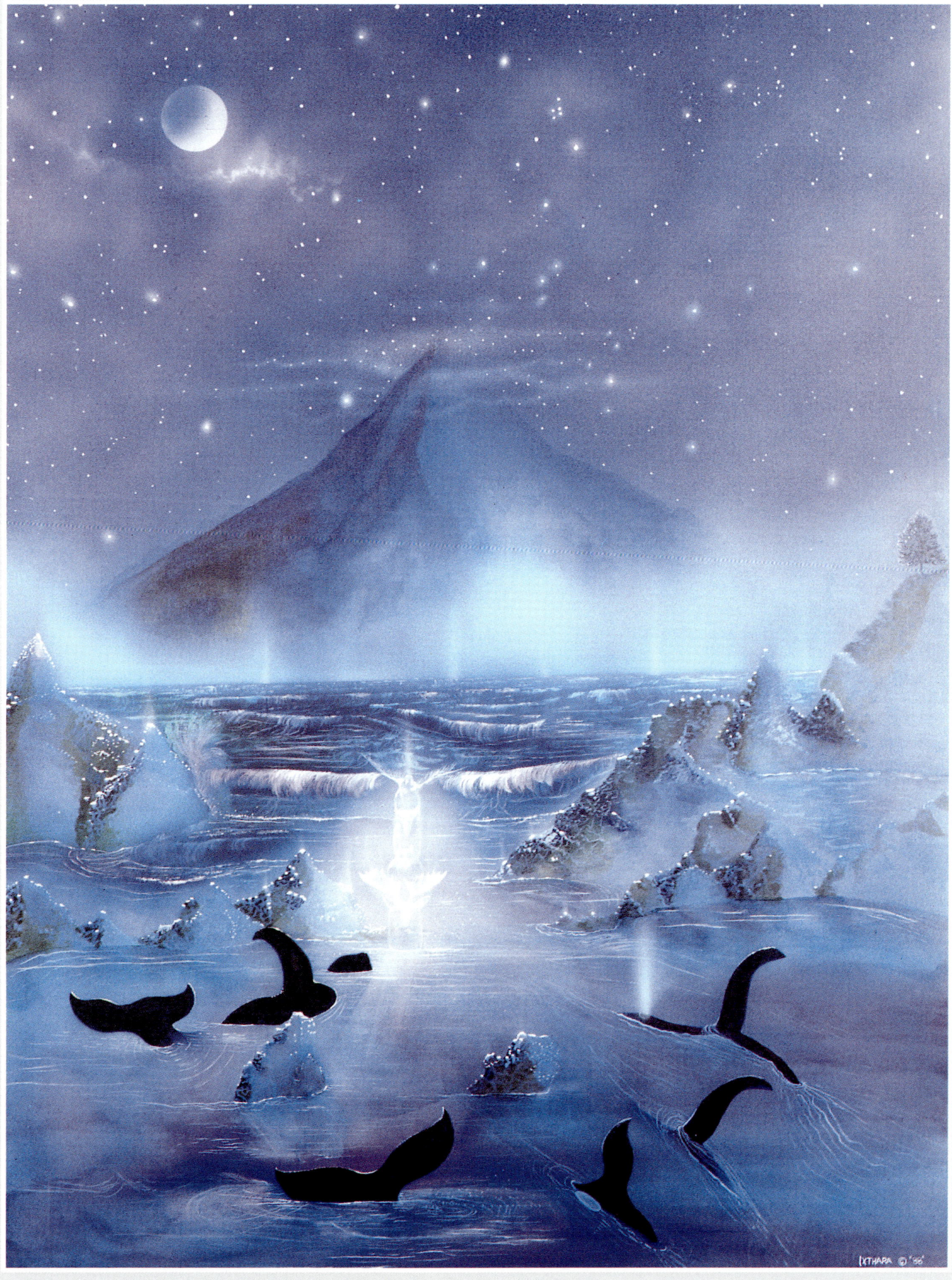
IXTHARA © '86

Angels of Atlantis
Ixthara

Distant Shore
Ixthara

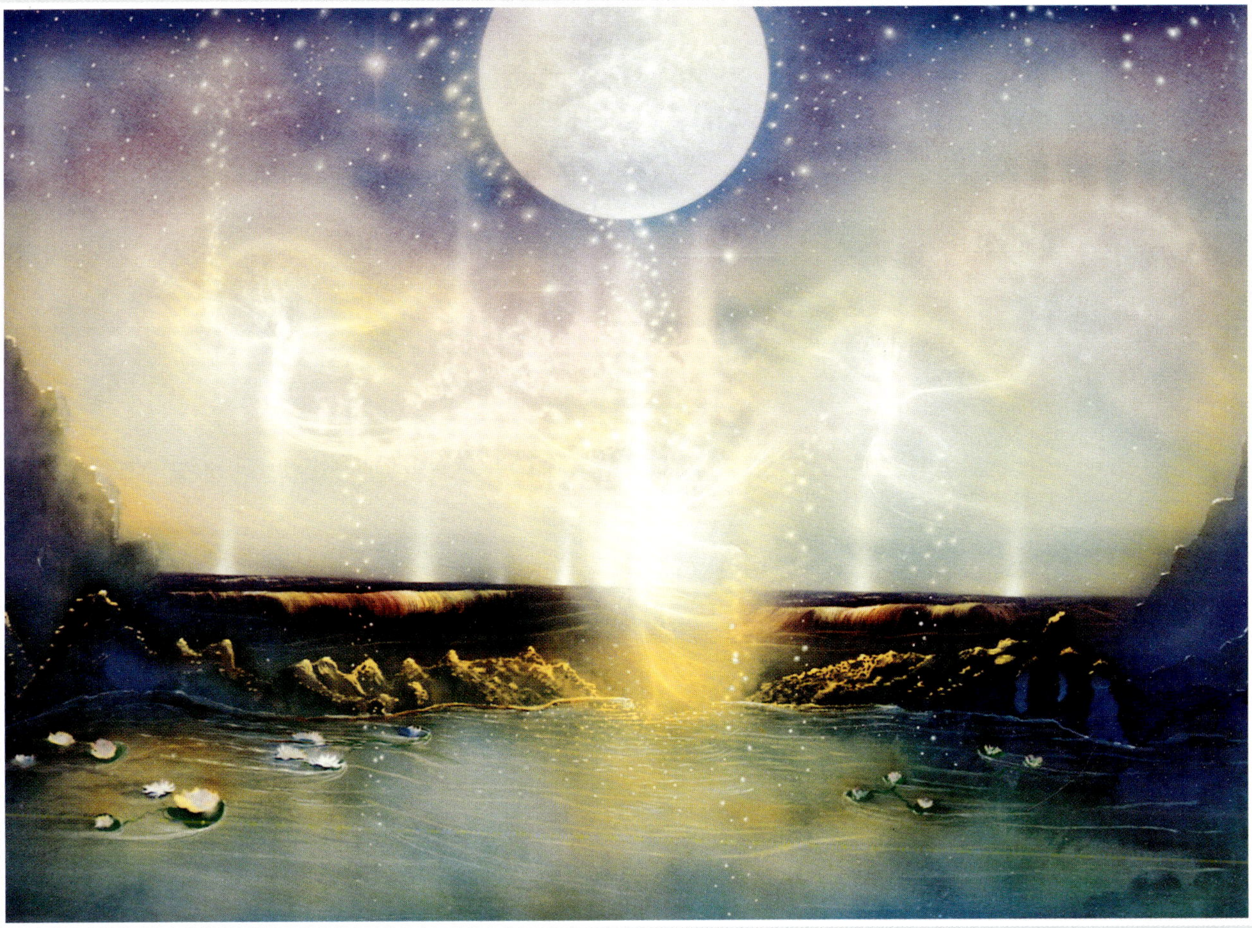

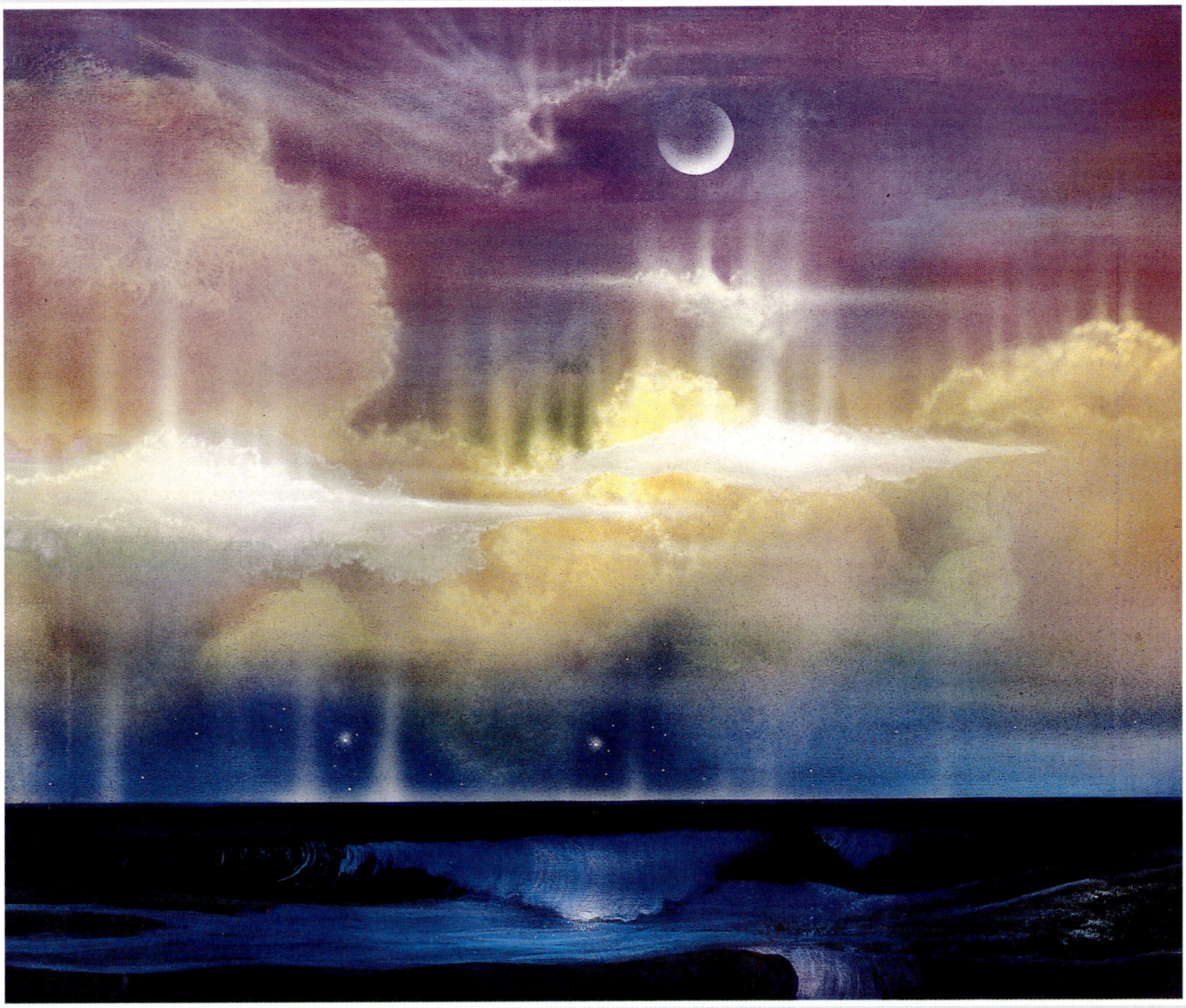

Rose Quartz Oracle
at Emerald Isle
Ixthara

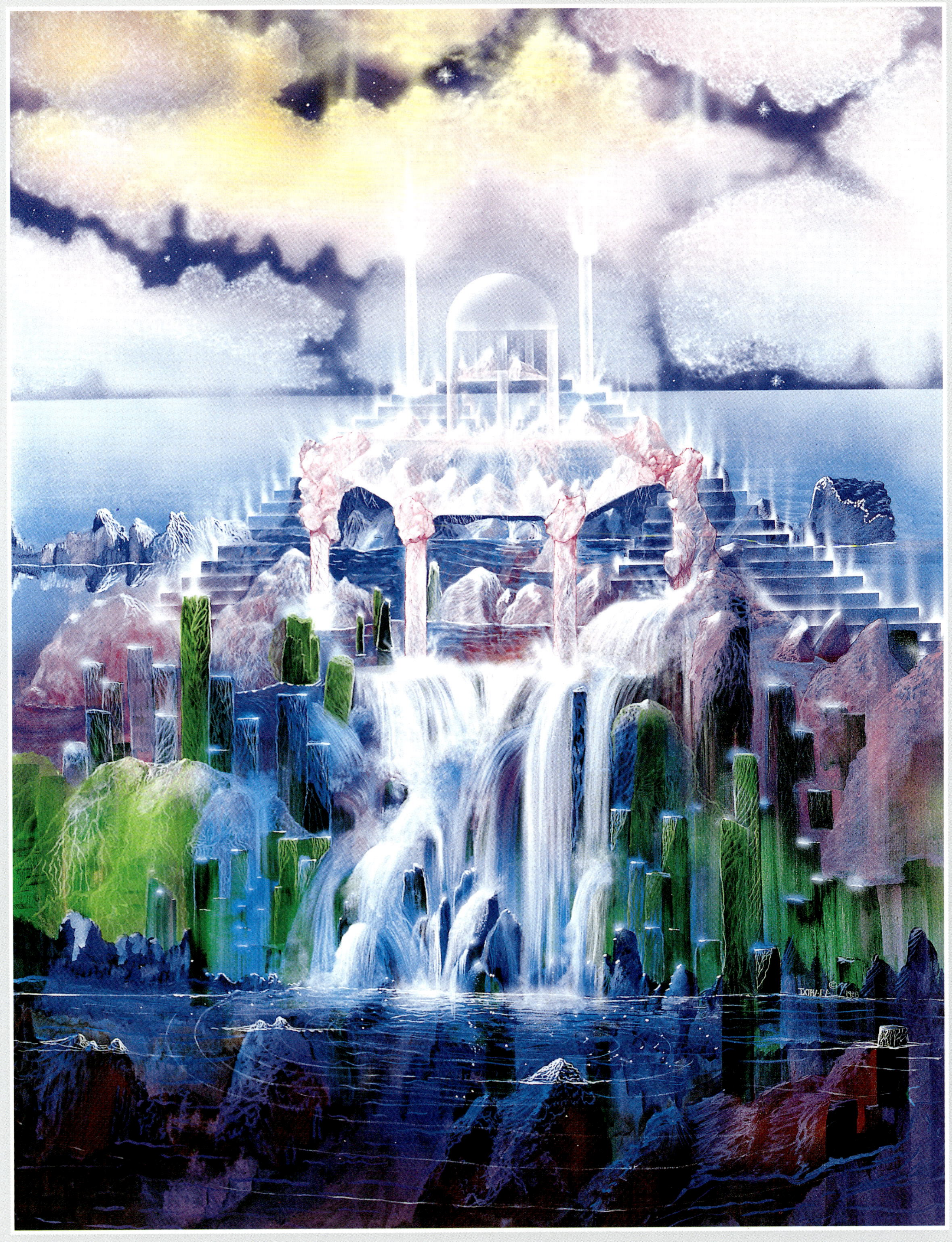

AEOLIAH

Aeoliah, New-age musician-composer, editor, and visionary artist has spent the last fifteen years devoting his time and energy to the healing arts. His primary form of creative expression during this time has been through his inspiring visionary art and through his healing music. His work is published and distributed throughout the world. Aeoliah's growing commitment to assist the healing and enlightenment of our planet is rapidly gaining him worldwide recognition as an inspired visionary at the forefront of our planetary evolution.

There is an inherent need in man for beauty. This need for the beautiful and sublime stems from his own quest for Self, and to discover the hidden mysteries of that reality which is unsullied by the perceptions of man.

Did you know that there are over approximately six million colors in the color spectrum, and there are only a very few that we can see and recognize in the rainbow that is visible to our visual perception?

Color and light have always been a fascinating subject for me. Ever since I was a child, color always attracted my attention, and it is only later in life that I realized the healing qualities of color and light. During my university studies in fine art, I wanted to explore the subtle mechanics of light and color and how light defines form and reflects the many changing colors in nature. I became very interested in studying how light shines through a crystal, and the different rainbow spectrums it created. After graduation and years of meditation and studying the dynamics of color harmony in our visible spectrum, I became aware of new color frequencies and new forms that have not been seen yet in this physical dimension. As my pituitary and pineal gland became increasingly activated, I started to

The New Birth
Aeoliah

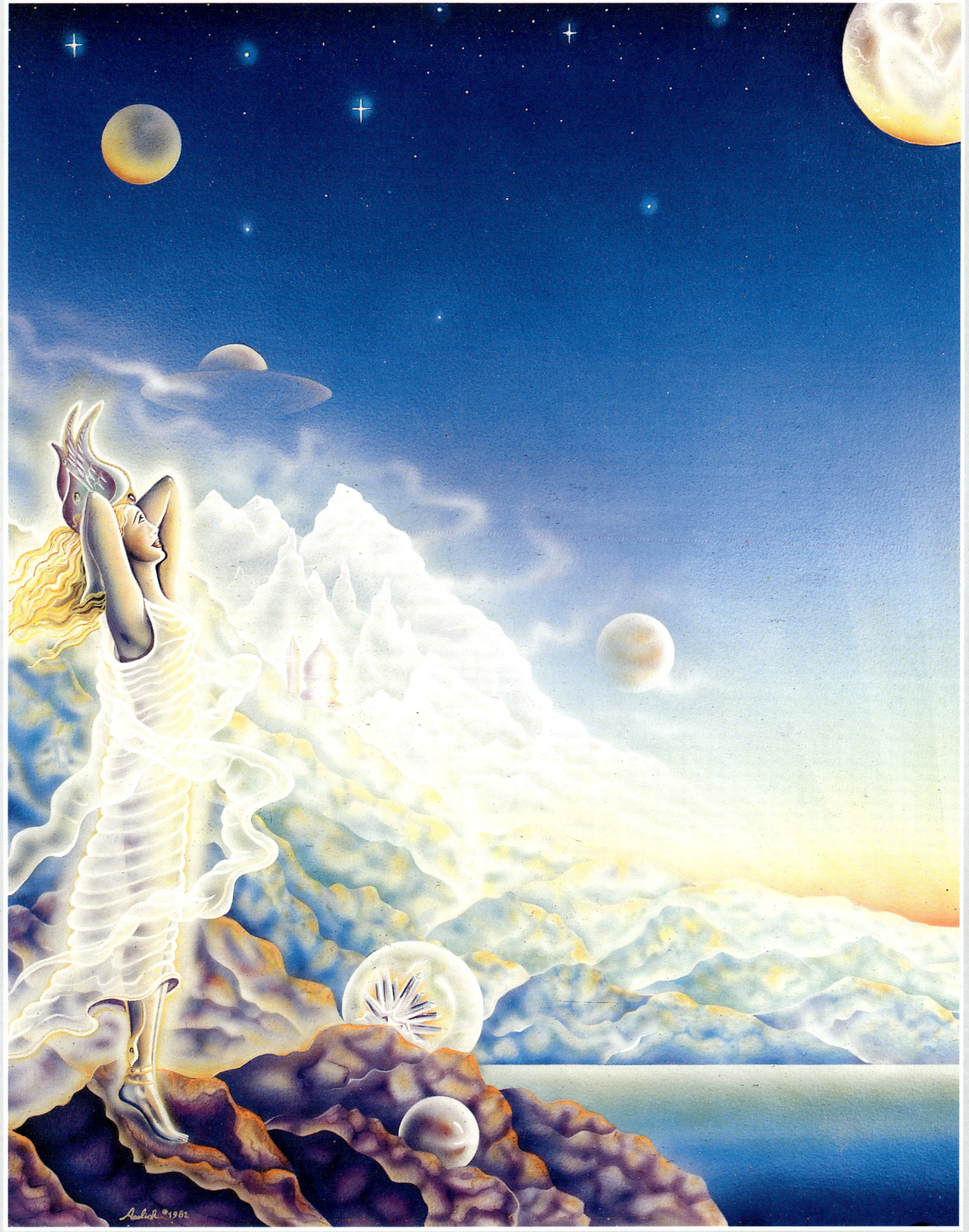

to experience new radiant colors and beings that were made of light, whose bodies were translucent with a shining radiance. These beings were so alive, radiant and beautiful that I recognized my calling to bring these healing images and colors into manifestation.

One of the specialties in the art I manifest, are a series of images of celestial beings who are serving and greatly assisting the evolution of our planet.

The emanation of these images progressively express a new shift in a universal awareness of Self as a radiant Light Force that sustains life after the so-called "death" of the physical body. These visions are here to remind us that there is only eternal life, and that so many beautiful dimensions exist, awaiting to enfold, embrace and welcome us home.

Visionary Art is an entrance into these dimensions where all our dreams and desires find their expression in the living canvas of our soul.

It is through the power of VISION that we learn how to be masters of manifestation and destiny.

Crystal Sage
Aeoliah

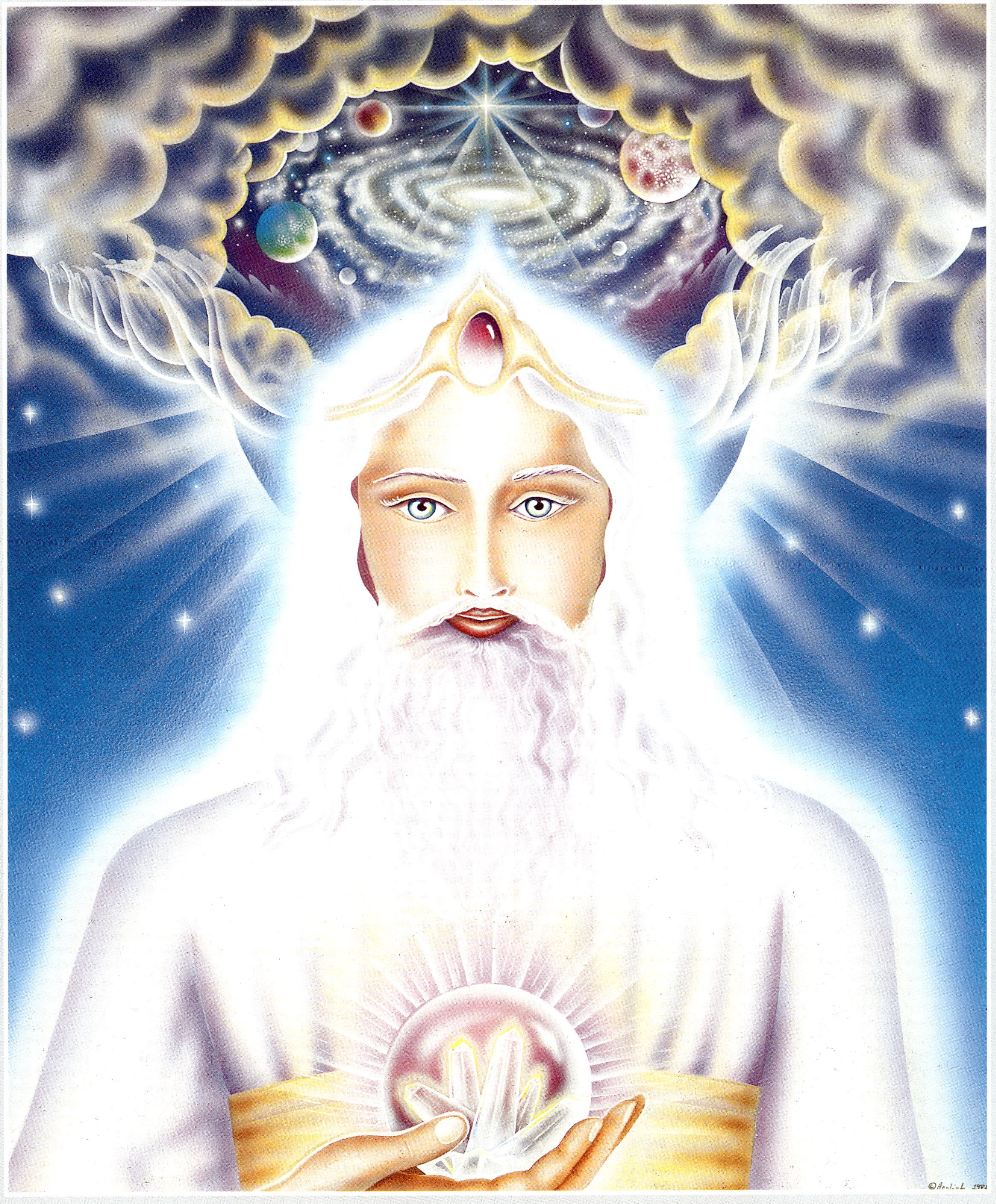

Crystal Goddess
Aeoliah

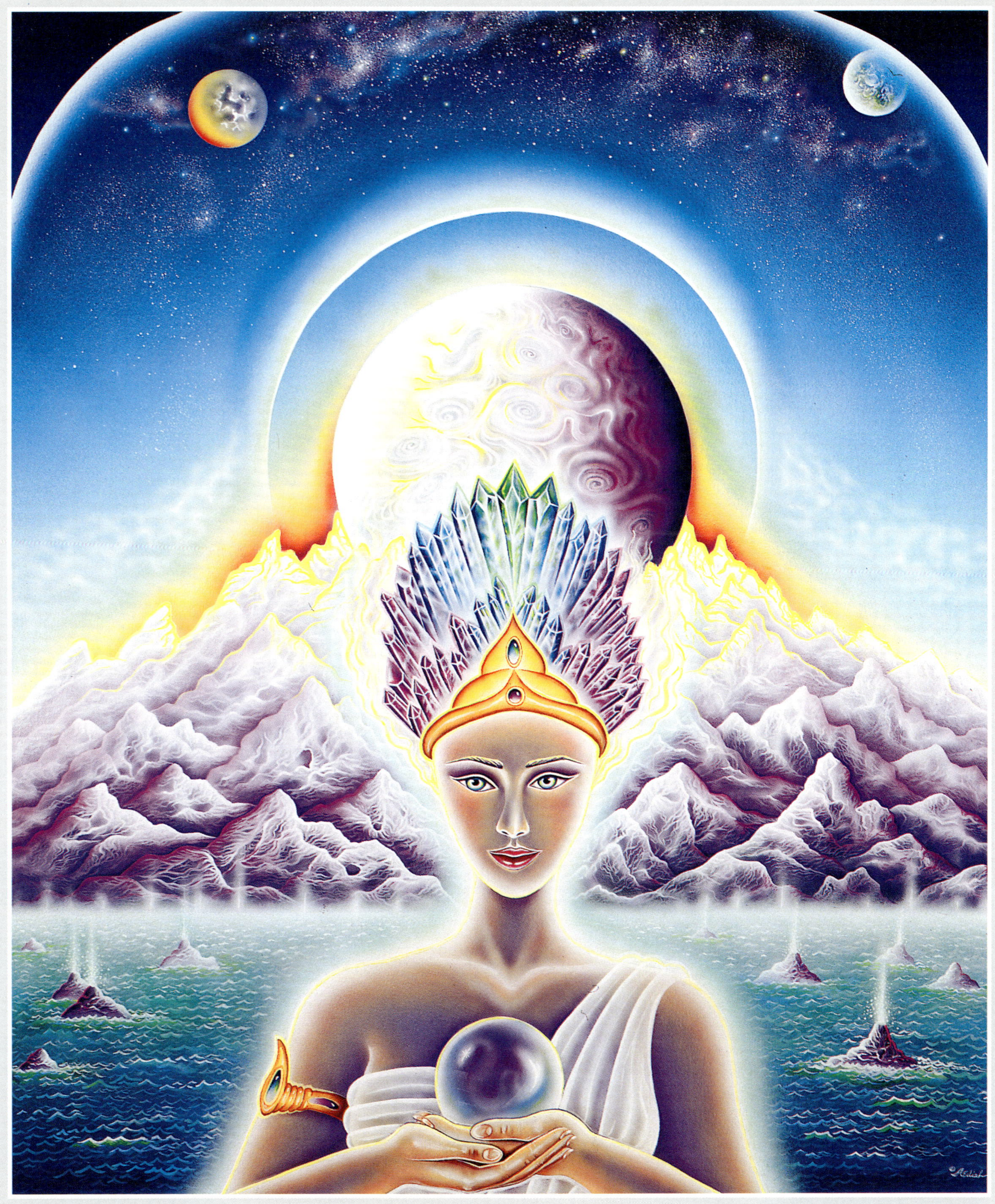

Music of the Spheres
Aeoliah

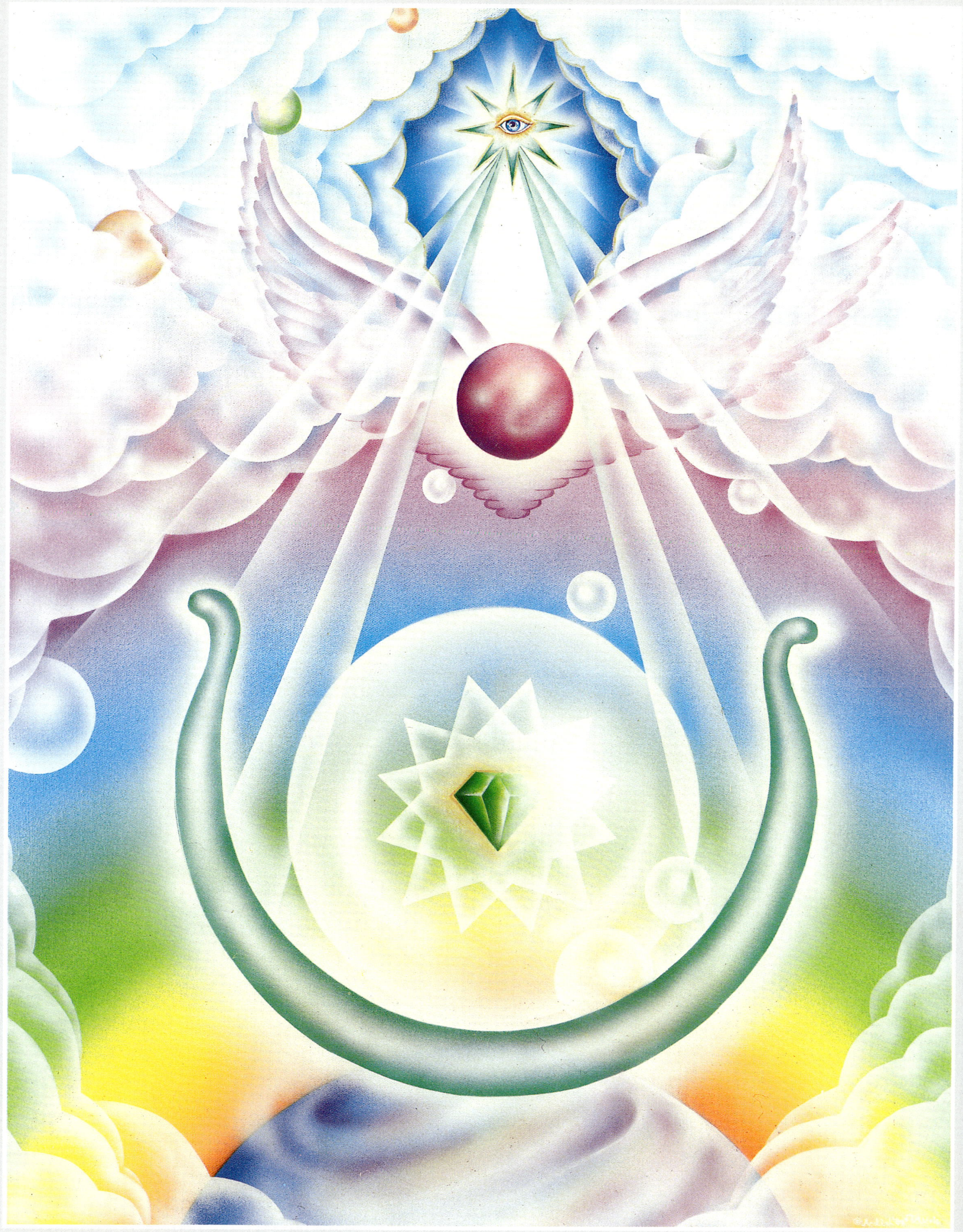

Angel of Illumination
Aeoliah

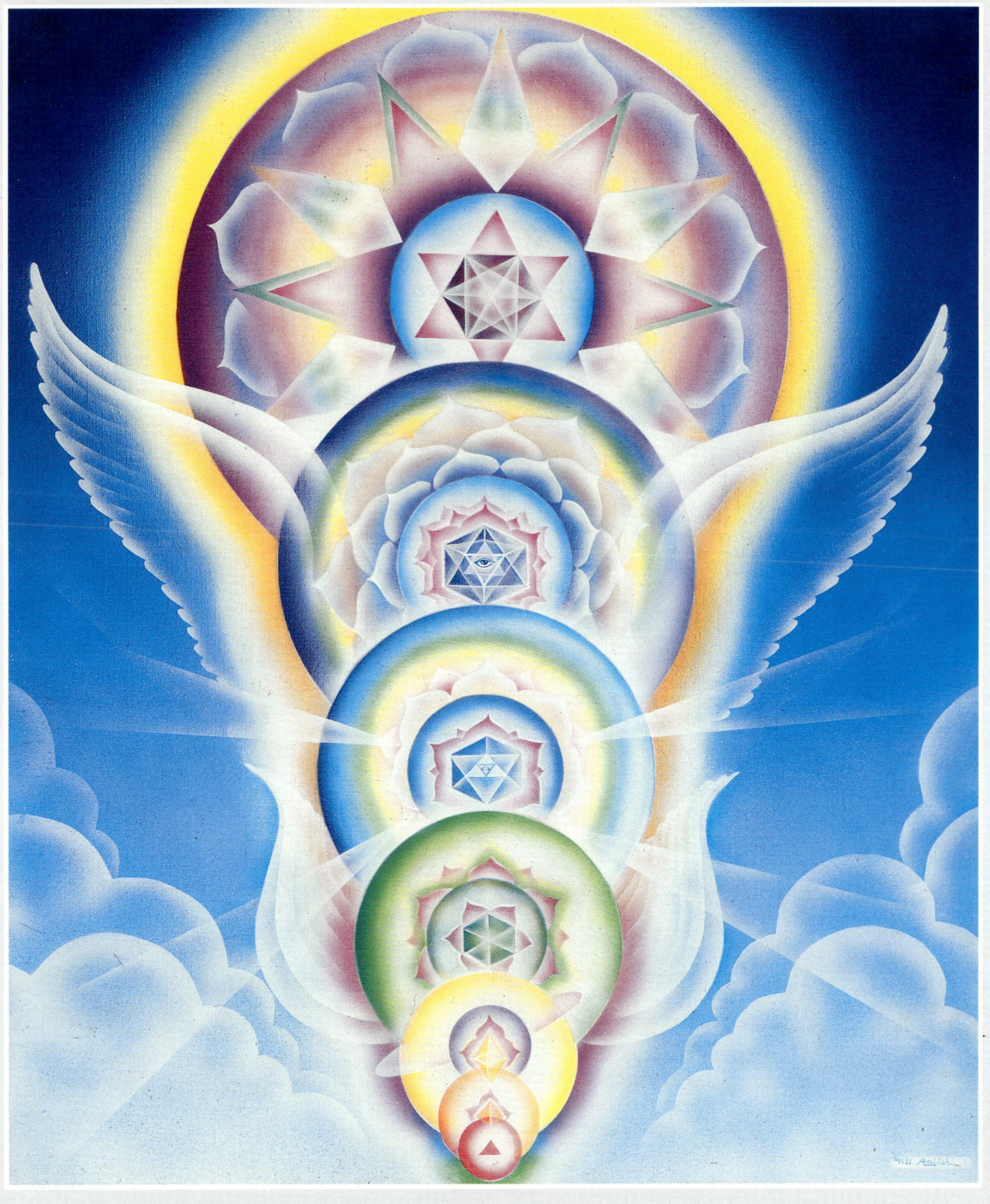

Krishna
Aeoliah

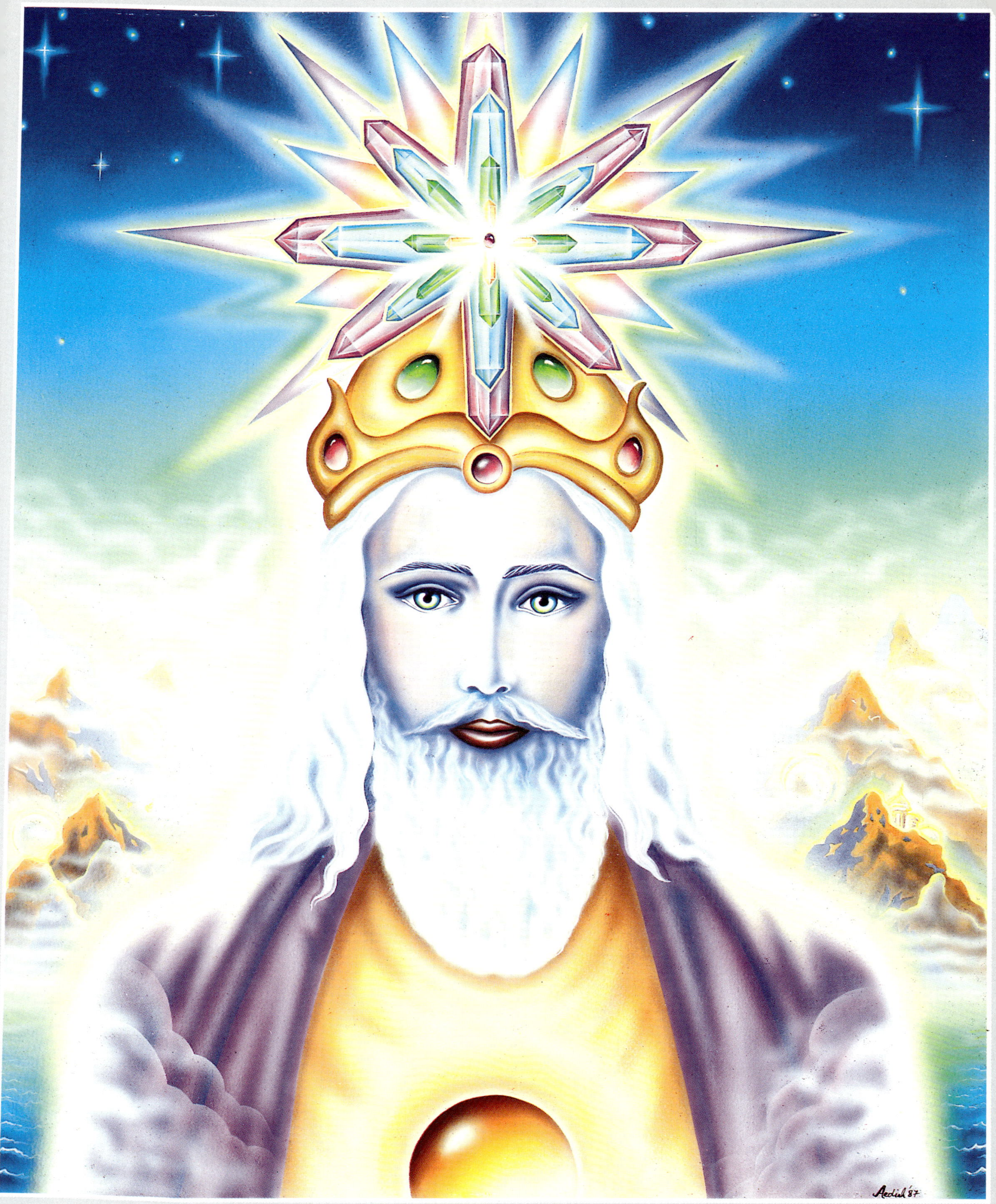
Aediel '87

Angel of Healing
Aeoliah